FOUNDATIONS OF PSYCHOLOGY

FOUNDATIONS OF PSYCHOLOGY

Instructor's Manual

Nicky Hayes and Paula Topley

LONDON AND NEW YORK

First published 1994
by Routledge
11 New Fetter Lane, London EC4P 4EE

Simultaneously published in the USA and Canada
by Routledge
29 West 35th Street, New York, NY 10001

Printed and bound in Great Britain by
Clays Ltd., St Ives PLC

British Library Cataloguing in Publication Data
A catalogue record for this book is available from the British Library

Library of Congress Cataloging in Publication Data
A catalogue record for this book is available from the Library of Congress

ISBN 0-415-11436-5 (instructor's manual – not available separately)
ISBN 0-415-11437-3 (overhead transparencies – not available separately)
ISBN 0-415-11024-6 (instructor's pack)

CONTENTS

LIST OF OHPs

INTRODUCTION

This instructor's manual is designed to help lecturers and teachers who are using "Foundations of Psychology" to teach introductory psychology. It aims to improve the student's understanding of chapter content, and to help lecturers and teachers in the assessment of written work, by clarifying the objectives underlying the student's learning. The set of OHPs provided is intended to be used in conjunction with teaching from the main text, and represent what the authors believe to be useful illustrations or tables emerging from the chapter content.

The manual's organisation reflects the chapter sequencing and content of "Foundations of Psychology". The manual is arranged chapter-by-chapter, so as to reflect the structure of the main text. Each chapter begins by highlighting key issues which arise from the chapters in the main text, and reproduces the chapter summaries from "Foundations of Psychology" in order to illustrate how those issues are addressed. The chapter summaries are also used to generate a set of learning objectives, which are intended to structure and direct student learning in these areas.

An objective question assessing each of the specified learning objectives follows. Together, these may be used in several ways: as self-assessment questions by students; as brief class tests on each chapter; or even collated by the lecturer to form a complete end-of-year test on the whole book. The objective questions for each chapter are followed by a set of revision and essay questions, and some suggestions for further reading. At the back of the book can be found answers to the objective questions, and some guidance notes which may be helpful when marking essays.

New lecturers or teachers seeking to appraise their students' learning may find it helpful to begin by using the objective questions, in order to provide a basis for the acquisition of factual information and knowledge. The revision questions can be used to help students to learn how to express their knowledge coherently, and how to organise it effectively. The full essay questions can then be used to teach students effective essay-writing skills.

Both experienced and new lecturers may find the learning objectives helpful in guiding student learning, and may wish to make these available to students for self-directed work. These learning objectives can also be used to generate further objective and revision questions, for use in teaching or in interim assessments taking place at the end of a period of teaching.

We have enjoyed compiling this manual, and believe that it could prove to be a helpful adjunct to teaching. So we do hope that you will find the material interesting, and useful.

Paula Topley & Nicky Hayes

March 1994

Our thanks are due to Dave Topley, for his help and support in the production of this manual.

CHAPTER 1   PERSPECTIVES IN PSYCHOLOGY

The key issues

In this chapter, we are looking at some of the basic assumptions which underly explanation and research in modern psychology. The changing schools of thought which form such a distinctive part of psychology's history are important, because each of them has left its mark on psychological methodology. Each new school of thought has brought with it different methods of studying the subject, and different assumptions as to what counts as valid knowledge.

The other main point which emerges from this chapter is the idea of triangulation: the use of different methods and approaches to investigate the same phenomenon. The psychological goal of understanding human beings can be tackled from many different standpoints, and these are to some extent reflected in the different areas of psychology. Each of them can tell us something different about the nature of the human being, and each has its distinctive approach to contribute to the whole picture.

Chapter summary

1. The philosophers Descartes and Locke, and the biologist Charles Darwin, were highly influential in setting the conceptual groundwork for the emergence of psychology as a discipline.

2. The early introspectionist psychologists studied the workings of the mind, by attempting to analyse their own and others' subjective experiences.

3. The behaviourist school of thought asserted that mental processes were unimportant, and that behaviour could be understood in terms of associations between stimuli and responses.

4. European psychology, such as the Gestalt school or the work of Jean Piaget, developed theories which were concerned with understanding mental experience and mental development.

5. The clinical origins of psychology included the psychoanalytic school of thought, based on the work of Freud, and later included behaviour therapy and humanistic psychotherapy.

6. The cognitive revolution re-introduced the study of the mind to psychology, but this time from an empirical, experimentally-based standpoint which emphasised how human beings process information. Other areas of psychology also began to acknowledge the importance of cognitive processes.

7. The modern emphasis on ethical issues in psychology brought with it an increased respect for the participant in psychological research, and a growing acceptance of non-experimental and qualitative research techniques.

8. Areas of psychological knowledge can be arbitrarily categorised into cognitive psychology, individual processes, physiological psychology, social psychology, developmental psychology and comparative psychology. But these categories overlap in many areas.

9. Perspectives in psychology include the issues raised by determinism, reductionism, interactionism, the nature-nurture debates, and nomothetic, idiographic and hermeneutic research.

LEARNING OBJECTIVES

1. **Philosophical perspectives**
    The student shall be able to:
    - identify major philosophical concepts in psychology
    - describe the theory of evolution
    - relate philosophical approaches to psychological theories

2. **Introspectionism**
    The student shall be able to:
    - name major early introspectionist psychologists
    - describe processes involved in introspectionism
    - identify limitations of the introspectionist approach

3. **Behaviourism**
   The student shall be able to:
   - identify major concepts in behaviourist thinking
   - relate the behaviourist approach to concepts of science
   - compare behaviourist and introspectionist approaches

4. **European psychology**
   The student shall be able to:
   - identify the basic assumptions of the Gestalt school
   - show how Piaget's approach links with evolutionary theories
   - contrast the European approach with behaviourism

5. **Clinical psychology**
   The student shall be able to:
   - identify sources of evidence in psychoanalytic theory
   - describe the basic assumptions of humanistic psychology
   - compare behaviouristic, psychoanalytic and humanistic
     approaches in psychology

6. **The cognitive revolution**
   The student shall be able to:
   - give reasons for the emergence of cognitive psychology
   - evaluate the computer metaphor in cognitive psychology
   - identify the cognitive approach in other areas of psychology

7. **Ethics and methodology**
   The student shall be able to:
   - describe assumptions underpinning ethical practices in psychology
   - show how ethical considerations have influenced psychological
     methods
   - relate ethical methodology to major areas in psychology

8. **Areas of psychology**
   The student shall be able to:
   - list the major areas of psychology
   - describe the major areas of psychology
   - compare major areas of psychology

9. **Perspectives**
   The student shall be able to:
   - define terms relating to psychological perspectives
   - identify the major nature-nurture debates in psychology
   - apply major perspectives to psychological theories

OBJECTIVE QUESTIONS

Philosophical perspectives

1. The _____ school of thought believes that there is no such thing as inherited knowledge

2. Darwin's theory of evolution is based on the theme of:
(a) survival of the largest
(b) survival of the fittest
(c) survival of the weakest
(d) survival of the most dominant

3. Locke's empiricism was the foundation for the psychological school of thought known as _____

Introspectionism

4. The first psychological laboratory was opened in 1879 by _____

5. The method known as introspection always involves:
(a) controlled experimental procedures
(b) controlled observational procedures
(c) reporting own experiences
(d) hypotheses about the mind

6. Watson criticised _____ because he said it was not scientific

Behaviourism

7. Skinner's approach to learning is known as _____ conditioning

8. According to Watson, the basic unit of learning was the _____ link

9. Introspectionism is different from behaviourism because:
(a) it deals with mental processes
(b) it does not use experiments
(c) it only studies behaviour
(d) it is concerned with animals as well as human beings

European psychology

10. _____ psychology took the whole person as its starting point

11. Piaget believed that the development of the individual re-traced the evolution of the _____

12. The European approach was different from behaviourism because:
(a) it involved the study of animals
(b) it used experiments as well as observation
(c) it was concerned with learning
(d) it emphasised theory

Clinical psychology

13. Psychoanalytic approaches to evidence are based on the idea of psychological _____

14. The _____ psychologists emphasised the idea of personal growth

15. Both psychoanalytic and humanistic psychology use the idea of:
(a) stimulus-response learning
(b) defence mechanisms
(c) modelling
(d) sustained attention

The cognitive revolution

16. Which of the following was not a factor in the origins of cognitive psychology?
(a) dissatisfaction with behaviourism
(b) war technology
(c) the development of computers
(d) the lack of previous experimental research in psychology

17. The computer approach to cognition is limited because:
(a) it is too hard for lay people to understand
(b) it disregards social and individual influences
(c) people don't like being compared with computers
(d) computers are more complex than the human brain

18. How people think about social experience is known as social _____

Ethics and methodology

19. The manipulative approach to "subjects" has been replaced by:
(a) respect for research participants
(b) increased use of animals
(c) brain scans and injections
(d) detailed standardised instructions

20. _____ methods in psychology have become important as a result of ethical concerns

21. As a result of ethical concerns, the _____ approach to studying animals has become increasingly important in comparative psychology

22. The study of human beings interacting with one another is known as:
(a) comparative psychology
(b) cognitive psychology
(c) physiological psychology
(d) social psychology

23. Developmental psychology includes the study of development through the _____ as well as in childhood

24. Developmental and comparative psychologists both study behaviour in the _____ environment

25. Nomothetic perspectives are concerned with:
(a) identifying general laws or principles about behaviour
(b) taking a single level of explanation only
(c) studying the individual
(d) identifying causes

26. The question of whether children learn to speak without help is known as the nature-nurture debate on:
(a) perception
(b) intelligence
(c) language
(d) schizophrenia

27. The idea that aggression is caused by genes is an example of a _____ theory

REVISION QUESTIONS

1. *Briefly describe the theory of evolution*

2. *Outline the major areas of psychology*

3. *What is meant by the term nature-nurture debate?*

ESSAY QUESTIONS

1. *Discuss the relationship between psychology's history and its methodology*

2. *How has the modern concern with ethical issues influenced psychological methodology?*

3. *How does the concept of levels of explanation help us to understand psychological issues?*

USEFUL FURTHER READING

Bell, P. B. & Staines, P. J. (1981) *Reasoning and argument in psychology* London: Routledge & Kegan Paul

Medcof, J. & Roth, J. (1979) *Approaches to psychology* Milton Keynes: Open University Press

Stratton, P. & Hayes, N. (1993) *A students dictionary of psychology* (2nd ed.) London: Edward Arnold

CHAPTER 2   PERCEPTION

The key issues

In this chapter, we are looking at perception, and in particular what it is and how it works. One of the most important features of this topic is the distinction between bottom-up (data-driven) models of perception, and top-down (theory-driven) models. The two types of theory emphasise different aspects of perception: typically, bottom-up theories deal with factual, veridical aspects of perception like that involved in identifying a specific object, whereas top-down theories emphasise active perception, and the way that the individual's ideas, expectations and assumptions influence how they perceive events or ambiguous stimuli.

It is a mistake, however, to see this as an either-or question, since perception isn't a single "thing". Rather, it is a complex of different mechanisms and processes, some of which are relevant for some types of perceiving while others are relevant for other types. Both kinds of theory can help us to understand what is going on. The final theory in the chapter, Neisser's perceptual cycle, can be seen as a synthesis of the two approaches.

Chapter summary

1. Perception is the process of interpreting sensory experience. We automatically tend to organise sensory visual experience into figures against backgrounds, and to use monocular and binocular depth cues to perceive distance.

2. Explanations for pattern-recognition include template-matching theories, prototype theories, and distinctive-features theories. The pandemonium theory shows how a distinctive-features approach may be applied to word-recognition.

3. Bottom-up theories of perception are those which argue that perception results purely from the stimuli available. These include the pandemonium model, Marr's computational theory of object recognition, and Gibson's ecological theory of direct perception.

4. The process of recognising faces includes both top-down and bottom-up processing. Research suggests that several different cognitive mechanisms may be involved in face recognition.

5. Top-down theories of perception are those which emphasise the importance of prior knowledge and other cognitive factors in directing perception. Perceptual set is the name given to a state of readiness to perceive certain things rather than others. It can result from knowledge, expectations and current circumstances.

6. Gregory's theory of perception proposes that perception results from hypothesis-testing. The hypotheses are derived from experience and perceptual principles. It is therefore a top-down theory of perception.

7. Studies of sustained attention found that performance decrements over time were reduced by situational, task and personal variables, and might be influenced by the individual's habitual level of arousal.

8. Studies of selective attention resulted in filter theories and limited-capacity models, but research into divided attention showed that with practice it is possible to learn to attend to more than one thing at a time, which challenges single-channel and limited-capacity models.

9. Neisser proposed that perception was a skill, involving an active cycle which combines both top-down and bottom-up elements. Anticipatory schemata direct perceptual exploration of the environment. This results in a perceptual sampling of the information available, which in turn influences the anticipatory schemata.

LEARNING OBJECTIVES
1. **Organising sensory experience**
   The student shall be able to:
   - describe basic features of perceptual organisation
   - link perceptual organisation with perceptual processes
   - analyse visual illusions in terms of perceptual organisation

2. **Explaining pattern recognition**
   The student shall be able to:
   - describe major approaches to pattern recognition
   - identify relevant applications of pattern recognition
   - evaluate models of pattern recognition

3. **Bottom-up theories of perception**
   The student shall be able to:
   - define "bottom-up theory" and give relevant examples
   - outline specific bottom-up theories of perception
   - evaluate the bottom-up approach to perception

4. **Face recognition**
   The student shall be able to:
   - describe a study relating to face recognition
   - distinguish between the processes involved in recognition of familiar and unfamiliar faces
   - identify top-down and bottom-up elements in face recognition

5. **Active perception**
   The student shall be able to:
   - outline a study illustrating perceptual set
   - identify individual and motivational influences on perception
   - apply the concept of perceptual set to everyday experience

6. **Gregory**
   The student shall be able to:
   - describe Gregory's theory of perception
   - compare perceptual and scientific hypotheses
   - relate visual illusions to cognitive strategies

7. **Sustained attention**
   The student shall be able to:
   - define terms relating to sustained attention
   - list the major factors influencing vigilance
   - describe the arousal explanation for sustained attention

8. **Selective attention**
   The student shall be able to:
   - define terms relating to selective attention
   - outline the major models of selective attention
   - relate empirical evidence to theoretical models of selective attention

9. **Neisser's perceptual cycle**
   The student shall be able to:
   - define terms relating to Neisser's perceptual cycle
   - describe Neisser's theory of perception
   - relate the perceptual cycle to everyday experience

OBJECTIVE QUESTIONS

Organising perception

1. Which Gestalt principle of perceptual organisation is illustrated by the following?   oooxxxoooxxxoooxxx

2. Which of the following is the basis for recognising objects?
(a) gradient of colour
(b) height in plane
(c) gradient of texture
(d) figure-ground organisation

3. Gregory explained the Müller-Lyer illusion as inappropriate _____

Pattern recognition

4. The theory in which patterns are matched up to a typical example is the _____ theory

5. Which of the following is the best example of pattern-recognition?
(a) recognising people
(b) reading
(c) holding a conversation
(d) catching a bus

6. There are difficulties with the template-matching approach because:
(a) it is too flexible
(b) it cannot distinguish templates
(c) it cannot explain reading handwriting
(d) it lists too many stimulus features

Bottom-up theories

7. Which is the odd-one-out?
(a) Marr
(b) Gibson
(c) Gregory
(d) Selfridge

8. The theory of perception which includes the idea of the $2^1/_2$D sketch is known as the _____ theory

9. Bottom-up theories of perception do not explain how we:
(a) identify objects
(b) see movement
(c) recognise words and letters
(d) understand social signals

Face recognition

10. Bruyer et al. studied a patient who:
(a) could not copy drawings of faces
(b) was able to describe faces in words
(c) could not recognise facial expressions
(d) could not recognise familiar people

11. Recognising familiar faces is unlike identifying unfamiliar ones because it sometimes involves _____ contexts

12. Infants seem to be pre-programmed to:
(a) respond to any face-like stimuli
(b) respond only to familiar faces
(c) respond only to unfamiliar faces
(d) ignore unfamiliar people

Active perception

13. Gilchrist and Nesburg found that hungry people saw pictures of food as:
(a) brighter
(b) less colourful
(c) extremely detailed
(d) larger

14. Taking longer to recognise an upsetting word is an example of _____

15. Particularly noticing dogs in the street because you are scared of them is an example of _____

Gregory

16. Gregory believed that perception involved _____ testing

17. Both perceptual and scientific hypotheses allow us to _____ from the immediate data to our wider experience

18. Gregory suggested that the Müller-Lyer illusion comes from:
(a) inadequate depth perception
(b) inappropriate constancy scaling
(c) monocular vision
(d) motion parallax

Sustained attention

19. Making more mistakes as time goes on is known as performance _____

20. Performance decrement is reduced by:
(a) monotonous signals
(b) the absence of other people
(c) environmental noise
(d) preventing feedback

21. The _____ law of arousal suggests that highly neurotic people will be less likely to miss signals if they are calmer

Selective attention

22. A _____ listening task involves a different message simultaneously in each ear

23. Triesman's theory of selective attention is also known as:
(a) the filter theory
(b) the bottleneck theory
(c) the pandemonium model
(d) the attentuation model

24. Broadbent's physical filter model was challenged by the _____ phenomenon

The perceptual cycle

25. The pre-existing ideas and expectations which we bring to perception form the _____ schema

26. Neisser regarded perception as:
(a) an innate ability
(b) hypothesis-testing
(c) a passive process
(d) a skilled activity

27. Noticing approaching cars rather than anything else when crossing the road is an example of _____ the visual environment

REVISION QUESTIONS

1. *What depth cues can be used to explain the Ponzo illusion?*

2. *Briefly describe the template-matching approach to pattern recognition*

3. *Outline the main stages involved in perceiving a tree, according to Marr*

ESSAY QUESTIONS

1. *What evidence do we have for the idea that figure-ground perception may be innate?*

2. *What can theories of pattern-rcognition tell us about the process of reading?*

3. *Do bottom-up theories of perception really explain perception? Give specific examples*

USEFUL FURTHER READING

Gregory, R. L. (1989) *Eye and brain* (4th ed.) London: Weidenfeld

Bruce, V. & Green, P. (1985) *Visual perception: physiology, psychology and ecology* Hove: Lawrence Erlbaum Associates

Neisser, U. (1976) *Cognition and reality* San Francisco: W. H. Freeman

CHAPTER 3   MEMORY

The key issues

One of the important issues which arises from this chapter is whether the process of memory itself can be separated from the human being who is doing the remembering. The concept of memory as an active process links with levels of processing theory to suggest that the active involvement of the person is an unavoidable ingredient in remembering. Mnemonic strategies can be construed as ways of forcing active involvement.

By contrast, assumptions of memory as a veridical recording are implicit in the two-process and working memory models. The computer analogy leaves little room for the idea that human beings are actively involved in adjusting and utilising what they remember, and treats that whole question as if it were entirely irrelevant. The study of memory as a whole, therefore, raises questions as to just how useful computer analogies of storage and immediate memories are to our understanding of how memory works in everyday living.

Chapter summary

1. Towards the end of the last century, Hermann Ebbinghaus developed a rigorous experimental paradigm for the study of memory, which continued to influence memory research throughout the 20th century.

2. Bartlett founded a tradition of investigating memory as an active process. Using serial reproduction, he showed how the schemata which people already possess influence and sometimes change what they remember. This led to research into confabulation and the influence of personal factors in memory.

3. Forgetting may occur as a result of decay of the memory trace, brain damage or disease, motivation, interference from other material, inadequate cues and contexts, or inadequate processing.

4. The two-process theory of memory sees memory as consisting of two qualitatively different types of store: an immediate, rapidly-fading short-term store and a long-term store for lasting memory. This was an accepted model of memory processes for most of this century.

5. The levels of processing approach challenged the idea that memory involves qualitatively different memory stores, arguing instead that the observed memory phenomena resulted from differences in the extent to which information had been processed.

6. The working memory model construed immediate memory and attention as involving a central processor with a number of peripheral devices designed to code or rehearse information.

7. Research into remembering in everyday life has included studies of prospective memory and metamemory, and of absent-mindedness. One significant distinction in absent-mindedness is between mistakes, which involve miscalculations, and errors, which involve performing an action inappropriately through lack of attention.

LEARNING OBJECTIVES

1. **Ebbinghaus**
    The student shall be able to:
    - describe Ebbinghaus' methods of studying memory
    - identify basic concepts in memory research
    - state limitations of Ebbinghaus' methodology

2. **Bartlett**
   The student shall be able to:
   - distinguish between the methods used by Bartlett and Ebbinghaus to study memory
   - identify changes which occur with serial recall
   - analyse the concept of memory as an active process

3. **Forgetting**
   The student shall be able to:
   - describe a study of forgetting
   - list theories of forgetting
   - identify factors which will minimise forgetting

4. **The two-process model of memory**
   The student shall be able to:
   - distinguish between long-term and short-term memory
   - describe a study of memory coding
   - evaluate the two-process theory of memory

5. **Levels of processing**
   The student shall be able to:
   - describe a study of levels of processing
   - explain the levels of processing approach to memory
   - show how levels of processing may apply to everyday life

6. **Working memory**
   The student shall be able to:
   - list the components of working memory
   - define terms related to the theory of working memory
   - describe a study of working memory

7. **Memory in everyday life**
   The student shall be able to:
   - define terms relating to everyday memory
   - describe significant concepts in the study of everyday memory
   - evaluate different methodologies for studying memory

Ebbinghaus

1. Ebbinghaus used _____ syllables to study memory

2. The form of remembering where someone is asked to identify a word they have seen before is known as:
(a) recognition
(b) redintegration
(c) serial recall
(d) re-learning savings

3. Ebbinghaus' methods were criticised because they lacked _____ validity

Bartlett

4. Unlike Ebbinghaus, Barlett deliberately used _____ material in his studies

5. Which of the following is not a usual outcome of serial recall?
(a) shortening
(b) coherence
(c) conventionality
(d) imagery

6. The study of _____ during wartime is a good example of serial recall

Forgetting

7. Milner's patient, H.M., suffered from _____ amnesia

8. Freud considered that all forgetting was really:
(a) retroactive amnesia
(b) the result of inadequate cues
(c) motivated forgetting
(d) proactive amnesia

9. Limiting the amount of _____ from other material can minimise forgetting

The two-process theory

10. The capacity for long-term memory is unknown, whereas the capacity for short-term memory is believed to be _____ items

11. Conrad found that STM mainly involved
(a) visual coding
(b) acoustic coding
(c) highway coding
(d) semantic coding

12. The two-process theory was criticised on the ground that both STM and LTM could be seen as different _____ of memory processing

Levels of processing

13. Which of the following was not used in Craik and Lockhart's 1972 experiment?
(a) polysyllabic coding
(b) auditory coding
(c) semantic coding
(d) visual coding

14. Information which involves a lot of mental work is considered to be _____ more deeply than information which is less significant

15. _____ fans remember that day's results better because they process them more deeply

Working memory

16. The working memory model includes:
(a) nonsense syllables
(b) confabulation
(c) the visuo-spatial scratch pad
(d) semantic processing

17. The articulatory loop involves:
(a) an internal voice
(b) a method of improving memory
(c) part of the auditory cortex
(d) the autonomic nervous system

18. Hitch and Baddeley found that people could do two tasks simultanously unless they both required _____

Memory in everyday life

19. A vivid memory of the context in which important events were learned is known as a _____ memory

20. Prospective memory involves:
(a) remembering to do things
(b) looking for information
(c) identifying appropriate solutions
(d) memory loss with ageing

21. An advantage of the diary method for studying everyday memory is that:
(a) it is not controlled
(b) it has ecological validity
(c) it can be difficult to analyse
(d) it is easy to carry out

REVISION QUESTIONS

1.   *What are the main changes which occur with serial recall?*

2.   *Outline the main explanations for forgetting*

3.   *Describe the levels of processing theory of memory*

ESSAY QUESTIONS

1.   *Memory is inseparable from the person who is doing the remembering. Discuss*

2.   *Evaluate clinical and laboratory evidence for the two-process model of memory*

3.   *How has everyday memory been studied by psychologists?*

USEFUL FURTHER READING

Eysenck, M. (1993) *Principles of cognitive psychology* Hove: Lawrence Erlbaum Associates

Baddeley, A. (1983) *Your memory: a user's guide* Harmondsworth: Penguin

Cohen, G. (1989) *Memory in the real world* Hove: Lawrence Erlbaum Associates

CHAPTER 4   LANGUAGE AND LITERACY

The key issues

One of the major questions which arises from the psychological study of language and literacy is to do with the social contexts of knowledge, in the form of the relationship between language and thinking. While few would accept the strong form of the linguistic relativity hypothesis, the idea that the language that we use shapes and colours our thinking is inescapable, and lies at the core of objections to sexist and racist language.

The other issue which inevitably arises from this area, and to some extent follows from the previous one, is that of social labelling. Here, the question which needs to be addressed is how far social labels are used to preserve the status quo, both in society and for specific individuals, and to act against effective change. Labelling as an issue can be used to bring together such diverse areas as verbal deprivation, accent and dialect, the sexist uses of language, and dyslexia.

Chapter summary

1. Language is a communication system which operates through combinations of arbitrary symbols, often in conjuction with non-verbal communication. Research into language use in conversations has focussed on the use of discourse and metaphor and on the social and co-operative aspects of conversational exchange.

2. The strong form of the linguistic relativity hypothesis proposes that language determines thinking; its weaker form proposes that it provides a framework and channel which heavily influences thought.

3. Bernstein's verbal deprivation hypothesis distinguished between restricted and extended language codes, and suggested that the use of restricted codes limited access to certain forms of meaning. This argument was strongly challenged by Labov.

4. Investigations of social aspects of language use include research into the influence of accent and dialects, and into the cognitive influences exerted by the use of sexist language. Studies of memory for language shows that people tend to remember the meanings they have derived from the language rather than an accurate record of the words which were used.

5. Theories of reading skills have, at various times, portrayed reading as stimulus-reponse learning, as translation from visual to auditory stimuli, and as a selective search for meaning.

6. Fluent and novice readers have been shown to differ in several respects, including the interpretation of spelling and the use of visual cues and eye movements.

7. Social knowledge in the form of scripts and assumptions are important in understanding and remembering language.

8. Reading disorders can result from a number of social factors, including verbal deprivation, lack of role models, and heavy television viewing.

9. Dyslexia is usually divided into acquired dyslexia, which has an identifiable organic origin, and developmental dyslexia, which concerns children failing to learn to read. Psychological explanations for developmental dyslexia include difficulties in processing visual information, fatigue, and social labelling.

LEARNING OBJECTIVES

1. **Language and discourse**
   The student shall be able to:
   - define forms of communication
   - identify the four basic components of conversation
   - describe methods of discourse analysis

2. **Linguistic relativity**

The student shall be able to:
- define linguistic relativity
- distinguish between the strong and weak forms of the linguistic relativity hypothesis
- describe a study of linguistic relativity

3. **Verbal deprivation**

The student shall be able to:
- define terms relating to the verbal deprivation hypothesis
- distinguish between elaborated and restricted codes of language
- describe Labov's criticisms of the verbal deprivation hypothesis

4. **Social aspects of language use**

The student shall be able to:
- define terms associated with social aspects of language use
- describe a study of accent or dialect
- discuss how sexist language can influence people's thinking

5. **Theories of reading**

The student shall be able to:
- identify factors which can interfere with word-recognition
- list the major theories of reading
- outline the theory of reading as a selective search

6. **Reading skills**

The student shall be able to:
- define terms relating to the study of fluent and novice reading
- outline the basic processes of reading
- distinguish between fluent and novice readers

7. **Social influences on reading**

The student shall be able to:
- describe a study of scripts in reading
- show how social factors influence the process of reading
- identify cognitive and social benefits of reading

8. **Dyslexia**

The student shall be able to:
- distinguish between forms of dyslexia
- describe theories of dyslexia as a cognitive deficit
- evaluate the concept of dyslexia

OBJECTIVE QUESTIONS

Language and discourse

1. Communication without language is known as _____ communication

2. Which of the following is not a basic component of conversation:
(a) quality
(b) manner
(c) grammar
(d) relation

3. _____ coding is a way of looking at the reasons people give in conversation

Linguistic relativity

4. The linguistic relativity hypothesis states that _____ is dependent on language

5. The idea that language determines thinking is the _____ form of the linguistic relativity hypothesis

6. Farb found that _____ women living in San Francisco interpreted their lives differently depending which language they spoke

Verbal deprivation

7. Meanings which are specific to the context are known as _____ meanings

8. Elaborated codes are unlike restricted codes because they are:
(a) situation-dependent
(b) context-dependent
(c) context-independent
(d) realistic

9. Labov argued that it was the formal testing situation which made _____ children appear verbally deprived

Social aspects of language

10. A shared variation in how words are pronounced is known as an _____

11. Edwards found that student teachers rated children with regional accents:
(a) more positively than others
(b) less positively than others
(c) the same as others
(d) sometimes more positively than others

12. Morgan argued that the use of "man" as a generic term:
(a) clarifies our understanding
(b) is more convenient
(c) allows us to see relationships better
(d) distorts scientific understanding

Theories of reading

13. Major _____ distortions can disrupt reading

14. The idea that reading is like hearing spoken words is known as:
(a) reading as translation
(b) reading as stimulus-response
(c) verbal deprivation
(d) reading as selective search

15. Prior knowledge brought to reading involves conventions, _____ and context

Reading skills

16. A basic unit of written language is:
(a) a morpheme
(b) a phoneme
(c) a lexicon
(d) a grapheme

17. Maintaining _____ is important in being able to read fluently

18. Being aware of the sound of words is not necessary for _____ readers

Social influences on reading

19. In Pichert and Anderson's study, people taking different viewpoints on material they had already read:
(a) recalled the same information
(b) were unable to recall anything
(c) recalled new but relevant information
(d) confused two sets of information

20. Heavy television viewing can:
(a) improve reading skills
(b) encourage verbal deprivation
(c) stimulate positive use of imagination
(d) interfere with learning to read

21. Donaldson argued that reading helps children to develop _____ thinking

Dyslexia

22. _____ dyslexia arises as a result of injury or brain disease

23. One theory of dyslexia is based on the observation that dyslexics are slower at matching visual and _____ forms

24. A problem with the concept of dyslexia is that:
(a) it is easily used as social labelling
(b) there are too many kinds of dyslexia
(c) there are not enough specialists to study dyslexia
(d) dyslexia is very common

REVISION QUESTIONS

1. *What are the main concepts in the study of discourse and conversation?*

2. *Summarise the verbal deprivation debate*

3. *Describe the major theories of reading*

ESSAY QUESTIONS

1. *"The English language is loaded to ensure that women cannot be perceived as equal to men". Discuss*

2. *How useful is the concept of verbal deprivation?*

3. *Is learning to read a purely cognitive process?*

USEFUL FURTHER READING

Ellis, A. & Beattie, G. (1986) The *psychology of language and communication* Hove: Lawrence Erlbaum Associates

Kennedy, A. (1984) *The psychology of reading* London: Methuen

Bolinger, D. (1980) *Language: the loaded weapon* London: Longman

CHAPTER 5   THINKING AND REPRESENTATION

The key issues

One of the central themes in the study of thinking and representation concerns the computer metaphor. It is easy to make the assumption that formal logic is the most accurate procedure in rational thought, but is that assumption really justified. How far do human beings really think like computers, and are those occasions when they think demonstrably differently really "errors"?

The study of social scripts and schemas, as well as problem-solving, suggests that human thinking and computer logic are qualitatively different. There are many forms of representation, and a sizeable proportion of them draw on wider social knowledge and experience. It is possible to argue that the application of a broader social knowledge to problem-solving is a more rational procedure than a strict adherence to formal logic. The question, therefore, is whether it is helpful or not to apply the computer metaphor to the understanding of human thought.

Chapter summary

1. Representation is concerned with how information is contained within the mind. Research into representation includes the study of coding and imagers, word-recognition, cognitive maps, schemas, frames and scripts, and concepts.

2. Research into concept-formation included associationist, hypothesis-testing and prototype models. Rosch showed how action and concepts were closely linked.

3. Studies of human reasoning show that people apply social knowledge to problems, and may therefore appear to be making "errors".

4. Investigations of problem-solving identified a number of mechanisms which can limit cognitive flexibility, including learning sets, Einstellung, functional fixedness and groupthink. Divergent thinking,

lateral thinking and brainstorming have been seen as ways of increasing creativity in thinking.

5. Studies of decision-making have shown that judgements of representativeness, availability, anchoring and entrapment are heuristics which exert a powerful influence on the decisions which people make, as do the decision frames within which the problem is set.

6. Computer simulations of human problem-solving have involved the use of means-end analysis and heuristics to solve simple problems. Part of doing so requires protocol analysis, or identifying the different steps to be taken in solving a problem.

7. Research into artificial intelligence systems has involved the development of interactive programmes and expert systems, and the analysis of expertise.

LEARNING OBJECTIVES

1. **Representation**
   The student shall be able to:
   - identify different models of representation
   - describe a study of representation
   - apply models of representation to everyday life examples

2. **Concept-formation**
   The student shall be able to:
   - describe models of concept-formation
   - define terms relating to concept-formation
   - evaluate methods of studying concept-formation

3. **Human reasoning**
   The student shall be able to:
   - identify distinctive aspects of human reasoning
   - distinguish between human reasoning and formal logic
   - describe a study of human reasoning

4. **Problem-solving**
   The student shall be able to:
   - define terms relating to problem-solving
   - describe aspects of mental set in problem-solving
   - identify strategies for enhancing problem-solving

5. **Decision-making**
   The student shall be able to:
   - define terms relating to the psychological study of decision-making
   - analyse heuristics involved in decision-making
   - describe a study of decision-making

6. **Computer simulation**
   The student shall be able to:
   - define terms relating to computer simulation
   - describe basic concepts in computer simulation
   - identify limitations of computer simulation

7. **Artificial intelligence**
   The student shall be able to:
   - describe types of research into artificial intelligence
   - identify mechanisms involved in expert systems
   - distinguish between artificial intelligence and human expertise

OBJECTIVE QUESTIONS

Representation

1. Piaget considered that representation occurs through the formation of _____

2. Kuhlman found that children who used mainly visual imagery:
(a) could classify pictures into sets easily
(b) could not classify pictures into sets easily
(c) were good at imagining what things would look like
(d) could count the number of stripes on a cat's tail

3. Knowing what to do when you catch a bus involves using a bus-catching

_____

Concept-formation

4. Associationist models of concept-formation saw it as largely a matter of

_____

5. Rosch believed that concepts involved:
(a) stereotypes
(b) icons
(c) words
(d) prototypes

6. One problem with conventional approaches to concept-formation is that they:
(a) are all observational data
(b) are too ecologically valid
(c) are too laboratory-based
(d) only involve studies with adults

Human reasoning

7. Choose the correct statement from the following:
(a) it takes longer to process positive statements than negative ones
(b) it takes longer to process negative statements than positive ones
(c) positive and negative statements take the same amount of time to process
(d) human beings are not able to process negative statements

8. Computer logic is different from human reasoning because computers cannot draw on _____ knowledge

9. Wason showed that human beings look for:
(a) real-life instances
(b) confirming instances
(c) abstract instances
(d) disconfirming instances

Problem-solving

10. _____ was defined by Luchins as "a fixed habit of mind".

11. Mental set is a state of:
(a) mental readiness
(b) mental fixedness
(c) mental alertness
(d) mental arithmetic

12. _____ is a group-based technique for enhancing problem-solving

Decision-making

13. Being unable to get out of a situation because too much has already been invested in it is known as _____

14. Using base-rate information or not is part of the _____ heuristic in decision-making

15. Chapman and Chapman studied _____ correlation in decisions about psychiatric diagnosis

16. GPS is an abbreviation for:
(a) general problem system
(b) general programme system
(c) general problem solver
(d) general probability solver

17. The steps taken in solving a problem are known as _____

18. Unlike humans, computers can only solve:
(a) very well-defined problems
(b) very vague problems
(c) easy problems
(d) ambiguous problems

19. ELIZA is an example of research into _____ programmes

20. The database of an expert system is for:
(a) enabling the computer to make decisions
(b) making computer decisions more accurate
(c) enabling an expert to draw on a wider range of knowledge
(d) making expert systems easier to use

21. Human expertise is different from artificial intelligence because humans can use:
(a) detailed knowledge
(b) explicit knowledge
(c) implicit knowledge
(d) accurate knowledge

REVISION QUESTIONS

1. *Outline Rosch's theory of concept-formation*

2. *What are the main factors which inhibit human problem-solving?*

3. *Describe an artificial intelligence expert system*

ESSAY QUESTIONS

1. *How are social and personal factors involved in knowledge representation?*

2. *"Human beings approach problem-solving in an illogical yet rational way". Discuss*

3. *Can computers simulate human thinking?*

USEFUL FURTHER READING

Matlin, M. W. (1989) *Cognition* (2nd ed.) New York: Holt, Rinehart & Winston

Sternberg, R. J. & Smith, R. E. (1988) *The psychology of human thought* Cambridge: Cambridge University Press

Eysenck, M. W. & Keane, M. T. (1990) *Cognitive psychology: a student's handbook* Hove: Lawrence Erlbaum Associates

CHAPTER 6   INTELLIGENCE

The key issues

This chapter raises the whole question of how far psychological research is embedded in its socio-economic context, and whether there is any such thing as an "objective" psychologist, given that they are also people with their own ideas and opinions. By highlighting how research became distorted by prior political beliefs, the chapter shows how a lack of a systematic approach to obtaining balanced evidence in the early years proved no barrier to the development and social implementation of scientific theory.

In terms of the study of intelligence itself, the elusive nature of measurement and reliability raises the question of reification, and how far the term should really be treated as an adjective rather than a verb. Recent theories of intelligence avoided such debates, and instead addressed the relative isolation of intelligence research from other areas of psychology. Both Gardner and Sternberg produced theories which integrated evidence from other areas of psychology, and so were able to provide fresh insights into this field.

Chapter summary

1. The psychology of intelligence has developed in a highly political social context, as the outcomes of psychological research have been used as justification for social stratification, educational policy, and eugenics.

2. The first IQ tests were developed by Binet at the beginning of the century, and were aimed to identify those who would benefit from special schooling. Binet did not believe they could or should be used as classification.

3. The first IQ tests combined Binet's work with that of Galton, and were used to classify and compare individuals. This led to a number of questionable social applications.

4. Binet's tests had adopted the age-correlation method, but Spearman's work on factor analysis produced a new form of IQ testing, which led to debates about whether there was a general intelligence, as opposed to several specific skills.

5. Cyril Burt provided data on twin studies which were highly influential in the nature-nurture debate on intelligence, but which appear to have resulted from scientific fraud.

6. More reputable investigations of nature-nurture issues in intelligence include twin studies and adoption studies. Overall, these have produce results which are equivocal.

7. There are several possible criticisms of validity and standardisation in IQ testing, and also of cultural bias in IQ tests. Arguments that differences between black and white Americans arise from inherited factors were thoroughly discredited.

8. Theories of intelligence have tended to be of two kinds: those which see intelligence as an adjective, or a property of action, and those which see it as a reified, abstract entity. Gardner took the latter idea further, proposing that there may be several different, independent intelligences.

9. Sternberg proposed the triarchic theory of intelligence, which argued that any account of intelligence must incorporate three facets: contextual intelligence, experiential intelligence, and componential intelligence.

LEARNING OBJECTIVES

1. **Political issues & Binet**
   The student shall be able to:
   - describe the principles underlying the original idea of the Intelligence Quotient
   - list Binet's three principles of intelligence testing
   - analyse social and political factors in IQ research

2. **The early IQ tests**
   The student shall be able to:
   - describe characteristics of the normal distribution
   - criticise features of the early IQ tests
   - identify eugenic influences on early IQ research

3. **The concept of g**
   The student shall be able to:
   - define terms relating to the idea of general intelligence
   - describe Spearman's model of intelligence
   - identify weaknesses of the factor analytic approach to measuring intelligence

4. **Cyril Burt**
   The student shall be able to:
   - explain the concept of heritability
   - describe Burt's evidence for the idea of heritability in intelligence
   - identify factors which suggest that Burt's evidence was unreliable

5. **Twin and adoption studies**
   The student shall be able to:
   - explain the principles of using twin and adoption studies to investigate intelligence
   - evaluate the major twin studies of intelligence
   - describe an adoption study of intelligence

6. **Validity and bias in IQ testing**
   The student shall be able to:
   - define reliability, validity and standardisation in IQ testing
   - distinguish between within-group and between-group variance
   - identify sources of cultural bias in IQ testing

7. **Multiple intelligences**
   The student shall be able to:
   - describe major theories of multiple intelligence
   - list Gardner's seven types of intelligence
   - identify sources of evidence for Gardner's theory of intelligence

8. **The triarchic theory of intelligence**
   The student shall be able to:
   - define terms relating to triarchic intelligence
   - distinguish between subtheories of triarchic intelligence
   - describe the features of componential intelligence

Politics & Binet

1. Early IQ tests were based on the principle of _____ correlation

2. Binet's _____ principle was that IQ scores are not labels

3. A meritocratic system is based on the idea that:
(a) the poor should have high-status positions
(b) the middle class are more intelligent
(c) the working class are more intelligent
(d) people's position in society should reflect their ability

The early IQ tests

4. Which of the following describes a normal distribution curve?
(a) a non-symmetrical bell-shaped curve
(b) a non-symmetrical U-shaped curve
(c) a symmetrical bell-shaped curve
(d) a symmetrical U-shaped curve

5. The US immigration IQ tests were culturally biased because they only showed scenes reflecting:
(a) American lifestyles
(b) European lifestyles
(c) Middle-class lifestyles
(d) Working-class lifestyles

6. The idea that people of low intelligence should not be allowed to reproduce is known as _____

The concept of g

7. The concept of g refers to:
(a) specific skills
(b) IQ scores
(c) general intelligence
(d) good ability

8. Spearman believed that there were two types of intelligence: general and _____ intelligence

9. Gould showed that the _____ factor disappeared if vectors used in factor analysis were oriented differently

Cyril Burt

10. Burt believed that intelligent parents having intelligent children demonstrates _____ in intelligence

11. The correlation coefficient which Burt claimed to have found among separated identical twins was:
(a) 0.86
(b) 0.32
(c) 0.58
(d) 0.98

12. Oliver Gillie reported that Cyril Burt's research _____ could not be located

Twin and adoption studies

13. If MZ twins are brought up in different environments, differences in their intelligence are thought to arise from:
(a) innate intelligence
(b) nutrition
(c) environment
(d) personality

14. The Shields and Juel-Nielson twin studies suffered problems because:
(a) the twins' lives were too different
(b) the twins' lives were too similar
(c) the twins had never lived together
(d) the twins had always lived together

15. Snygg compared IQs of adopted and fostered children with their _____ mothers

16. If a test gives a consistent result it is said to be _____

17. Between-group variance refers to comparisons between:
(a) two very similar populations
(b) groups chosen from the same population
(c) comparisons between families
(d) two entirely different populations

18. Labov showed that differences between black and white Americans were likely to have arisen from _____ factors

19. Gardner identified _____ different types of intelligence

20. Which of the following was not included in Gardner's theory:
(a) intrapersonal intelligence
(b) mathematical intelligence
(c) historical intelligence
(d) interpersonal intelligence

21. Gardner drew on cases of _____ which affected specific mental functions

22. Becoming so practised at a skill that you don't have to think about it is known as _____

23. _____ intelligence is about how our own personal history affects how we do things.

24. Which of the following are not part of componential intelligence:
(a) metacomponents
(b) performance components
(c) knowledge acquisition components
(d) skill acquisition components

REVISION QUESTIONS

1.   *Describe the age-correlation approach to assessing intelligence*

2.   *What can twin studies tell us about intelligence?*

3.   *What are the three subtheories in the triarchic theory of intelligence?*

ESSAY QUESTIONS

1.   *"The development of intelligence testing directly contradicted Binet's original intentions". Discuss*

2.   *Discuss, giving evidence, the idea that intelligence is genetically determined*

3.   *Compare and contrast Sternberg's triarchic theory of intelligence with Gardner's multiple intelligence theory*

USEFUL FURTHER READING

Sternberg, R. J. (1985) *Beyond IQ: a triarchic theory of human intelligence* Cambridge: Cambridge University Press

Gardner, H. (1985) *Frames of mind: the theory of multiple intelligences* London: Paladin

Gould, S. J. (1981) *The mismeasure of man* Harmondsworth: Penguin

CHAPTER 7   THEORIES OF PERSONALITY

The key issues

More than any other topic, this one highlights the very different models of the human being which underpin differing schools of thought in psychology. The genetic determinism of early trait approaches contrasts with the social determinism of Bandura and Mischel, and the very different approaches presented by the psychoanalytic and humanistic schools, which contrasts again with the pragmatism of the narrow-band theories. Each different approach describes a very different human animal.

These contrasts also mean that differences in methodology and assessment come to the fore, since most of the theories of personality have involved some kind of personality assessment. Idiographic and nomothetic perspectives become highlighted in the kinds of outcomes which are produced by various kinds of personality test, as well as being emphasised in the content of the theories themselves.

Chapter summary

1. Early theories of personality include the cognitive, conative and affective personality domains, the theory of the humours, phrenology, and somatotypes.

2. Freud's theory of personality showed the ego maintaining a dynamic balance between the demands of reality, the id and the superego, with ego-defence mechanisms protecting the ego against threat from these sources. Early experiences in childhood could produce lasting effects on the adult personality.

3. Jung believed that human beings had access to a shared collective unconscious, which could operate in a healing way. Some everyday objects became invested with special significance because they were synchronous with archetypes in the collective unconscious.

4. Fromm believed society, as well as family and maturation, was important in shaping character. Different types of characters, either productive or negative, could result from the combined influences of any of these sources.

5. Eysenck proposed that the personality traits of introversion and neuroticism had a biological basis, which was genetic in origin. He believed that these two traits could be taken as accounting for the majority of individual differences in personality.

6. Cattell proposed that personality could be described as combinations of sixteen different traits, and that it was therefore necessary to emphasise the value of personality profiles rather than numerical scores.

7. Factor analysis of the outcomes of different personality tests revealed a consistent "five robust factors". There was some disagreement as to the exact content of each factor, but not much on the existence of the five themselves.

8. The behaviourist model of personality saw personality as simply resulting from combinations of stimulus-response connections, learned by the individual throughout life.

9. Social learning theory emphasised the importance of imitation in the acquisition of novel forms of behaviour, and of identification with role models in learning general styles. Together, these learning processes formed the foundations of individual personality.

10. Symbolic interactionism, as proposed by G. H. Mead, saw personality as a result of the social roles which the individual was required to play throughout life, and with which they were expected to interact.

11. Social cognitive theory argued that social-learning, expectancies, values and self-efficacy beliefs were sufficient to account for individual differences in personality.

12. Rogers argued that people had two basic needs: a need for self-actualisation and a need for positive regard from others. Both of these had to be satisfied for healthy personality development.

13. Kelly argued that people develop personal constructs - theories about reality which they use to make sense out of what happens to them. In order to understand someone's personality, Kelly believed that it was necessary to understand their individual personal construct system.

14. The authoritarian personality theory showed how a number of personality traits clustered together to make a particularly rigid and intolerant type of personality, which was particularly likely to engage in social prejudice and racism.

15. Type A and Type B personalities adopted different ways of handling competitive situations, which produced differences in the degree of personal stress and the rate of coronary failure.

16. Nomothetic theories of personality seek to compare people on general criteria; idiographic ones seek to describe the individual in depth. Normative psychometric tests are used for comparing different people, but ipsative tests look at the balance of different traits within the single individual.

LEARNING OBJECTIVES

1.   **Early theories of personality**
     The student shall be able to:
     - define terms relating to early theories of personality
     - describe early theories of personality
     - identify examples of personality types

2. **Psychoanalytic theories**
   The student shall be able to:
   - outline the major ego-defence mechanisms
   - evaluate the psychoanalytic approach
   - describe basic concepts in the psychoanalytic theories developed by Jung and Fromm

3. **Trait theories of personality**
   The student shall be able to:
   - describe trait theories of personality
   - define terms relating to trait theories of personality
   - evaluate the trait approach to personality

4. **Learning theories**
   The student shall be able to:
   - define terms relating to learning theories of personality
   - describe behaviourist approaches to personality
   - distinguish between imitation and identification

5. **Social cognition and symbolic interactionism**
   The student shall be able to:
   - outline Mead's theory of the social development of personality
   - describe concepts of symbolic interactionism
   - identify forms of expectancy in social cognitive approaches to personality

6. **Rogers and Kelly**
   The student shall be able to:
   - describe key concepts in Rogers theory of personality
   - define terms relating to personal construct theory
   - explain the phenomenological approach to personality

7. **Narrow-band theories**
   The student shall be able to:
   - list the personality traits of the authoritarian personality
   - distinguish between type A and type B personalities
   - describe a study involving a narrow-band approach to personality

8. **Perspectives**
   The student shall be able to:
   - define terms relating to approaches to personality and personality testing
   - distinguish between nomothetic and idiographic theories of personality
   - give examples of different types of personality theories

OBJECTIVE QUESTIONS

Early theories

1. Studying personality by examining the bumps on the skull was known as

_____

2. Kretschmer argued that personality was associated with _____

3. Sheldon believed that endomorphs were:
(a) insensitive
(b) easy-going
(c) intelligent
(d) sporty

Psychoanalytic theories

4. Forgetting an event because it is too traumatic is known as _____

5. It is difficult to apply Popper's principle of _____ to psychoanalytic theory

6. Fromm particularly emphasised the importance of
(a) early sexual experience
(b) society
(c) synchronicity
(d) the collective unconscious

Trait theories

7. Which of the following was not identified as a basic personality trait by Eysenck?
(a) introversion
(b) psychoticism
(c) romanticism
(d) extraversion

8. Tests designed to measure aspects of mental functioning are known as _____ tests

9. Claridge suggested that _____ was a more useful concept than personality

Learning theories

10. Theories which see just one level of explanation as all that is necessary are known as _____ theories

11. Skinner saw learning as happening through the law of:
(a) effort
(b) effect
(c) exercise
(d) equipotentiality

12. _____ involves copying specific actions from a model

Social theories

13. The _____ stage was the second stage of personality development identified by Mead

14. Symbolic interactionism is the study of:
(a) stimulus-response links
(b) roles in social life
(c) unconscious motives
(d) personal constructs

15. Beliefs about one's own competence are known as _____ beliefs

16. The need for self-actualisation is about striving for:
(a) perfection
(b) approval
(c) material success
(d) personal development

17. According to Kelly, the theories which people use to explain their experience are known as _____

18. The phenomenological approach emphasises:
(a) how people interact with others
(b) how people see their own situations
(c) people's unconscious motives
(d) nomothetic testing

19. Which of the following is not a trait of the authoritarian personality syndrome:
(a) destructiveness
(b) conventionalism
(c) anti-contraception
(d) authoritarian submissiveness

20. A highly competitive person is generally a Type _____ personality

21. Glass found that Type As became more stressed than Type Bs when they could not _____ situations

22. Tests which identify the relative balance of characteristics within a single person are known as _____ tests

23. Nomothetic theories look for things people have in common, but idiographic ones are more concerned with _____

24. Theories which locate the essence of personality in the unconscious mind are known as:
(a) humanistic theories
(b) behaviourist theories
(c) psychoanalytic theories
(d) phenomenological theories

REVISION QUESTIONS

1. *Briefly describe the model of personality proposed by either Jung or Fromm*

2. *Describe the sources of data which Cattell used in the development of the 16PF*

3. *Outline Rogers' theory of personality*

ESSAY QUESTIONS

1. *"Trait explanations of personality are intrinsically inadequate". Discuss*

2. *How far do the concepts of social learning, symbolic interactionism and social cognition make the concept of personality redundant?*

3. *Can phenomenological approaches provide us with a full understanding of personality?*

USEFUL FURTHER READING

Mischel, W. (1986) *Introduction to personality: a new look* London: Holt, Rinehart & Winston

Fransella, F. (1981) *Personality: theory, measurement and research* London: Methuen

Burr, V. & Butt, T. (1992) *Invitation to personal construct psychology* London: Whurr

CHAPTER 8   THE MEDICAL MODEL OF ABNORMAL BEHAVIOUR

The key issues
This chapter addresses the development of the medical model of abnormal behaviour. It begins by looking at the early forms of explanation for abnormal behaviour, showing how the concept of illness is a relatively recent development. It then goes on to describe two different classification systems within the medical model, and some of their associated problems and criticisms.

The chapter then goes on to examine ways of defining normality and abnormality, before looking at the three specific disorders of schizophrenia, depression and anorexia. Different theoretical explanations for these disorders are compared, together with their implications for therapy.

Chapter summary

1. Explanations for why someone is acting oddly have changed through the centuries. The medical model is the form of explanation current in modern society.

2. Systems of classifying mental illness began with a distinction between five kinds: neuroses, personality disorders, organic psychoses, functional psychoses, and mental retardation. This led to a number of problems with reliability of diagnosis.

3. The current system of psychiatric diagnosis is known as DSM-IIIR. It examines the problem by loooking at five axes: clinical syndromes, personality disorders, physical disorders, psychosocial stressors and adaptive functioning.

4. The medical model of abnormal behaviour results in somatic therapies, which involve chemical, electrical or physical forms of intervention with the body, designed to alleviate or cure mental disorders.

5. The medical model has attracted considerable criticism, notably from Thomas Szasz, who argued that problems in living was a more useful concept than mental illness.

6. Abnormality, as used by the medical model, is an elusive concept. It does not conform to statistical or normative criteria for abnormality, and may vary in social groups and cultures. Its conventional nature can lead to bias in psychiatric diagnosis.

7. Schizophrenia is an example of a specific mental disorder in the medical model. It has variously been seen as being "caused" by genetics, brain chemicals, family influences, and social stressors. The modern view proposes that these factors combine to make some people more vulnerable than others.

8. There are various kinds of depression, including bipolar depression, or manic-depressive psychosis, and unipolar depression. Depression may have its effect on moods, thoughts, motivations, and physical interactions like appetite. Cognitive, social and genetic explanations for depression have all been proposed.

9. Anorexia nervosa and bulimia are both eating disorders. Anorexia can ultimately result in the individual starving to death, and several possible causes have been proposed. Bulimia involves binge eating alternating with purges, and appears to be an obsessive form of neurosis.

LEARNING OBJECTIVES
1. **Historical approaches**
    The student shall be able to:
    - name historical theories of abnormal behaviour
    - describe early theories of abnormal behaviour
    - evaluate early therapies of abnormal behaviour

2. **Early classification systems**
    The student shall be able to:
    - identify underlying assumptions of the medical model
    - describe the different categories of mental illness
    - criticise the early classification system

3. **Somatic therapies**
   The student shall be able to:
   - describe early approaches to somatic therapy
   - list the three main approaches to somatic therapy
   - define terms relating to somatic therapies

4. **The medical model**
   The student shall be able to:
   - give reasons for the acceptance of the medical model
   - evaluate the concept of mental illness
   - discuss mental illness in its social context

5. **DSM-IIIR**
   The student shall be able to:
   - describe the five axes of DSM-IIIR
   - link problems of diagnosis to the emergence of DSM-IIIR
   - evaluate the medical approach of psychiatric diagnosis

6. **Normality and abnormality**
   The student shall be able to:
   - describe definitions of abnormality and normality
   - evaluate definitions of abnormality
   - list criteria for defining the concept of normality

7. **Schizophrenia**
   The student shall be able to:
   - list different types of schizophrenia
   - evaluate competing theories of schizophrenia
   - describe social mechanisms involved in schizophrenia

8. **Depression**
   The student shall be able to:
   - distinguish between different types of depression
   - describe a study of learned helplessness
   - discuss explanations of depression

9. **Eating disorders**
   The student shall be able to:
   - identify types of eating disorders
   - evaluate explanations for eating disorders
   - link eating disorders with models of abnormal behaviour

Historical approaches

1. Hippocrates was the first physician to see mental illness as having a _____ origin

2. An excess of black bile would produce individuals who were:
(a) nervous
(b) excitable
(c) aggressive
(d) depressed

3. Moral therapy became unfashionable because it was considered to be _____ in its approach

Early classification

4. The medical model assumes that abnormal behaviour comes from:
(a) symptoms following physical sickness
(b) malfunction in the brain
(c) poor social relationships
(d) disturbed families

5. A _____ is a person who has lost touch with reality

6. Kraepelin's system was criticised because:
(a) psychiatrists did not agree on diagnosis
(b) psychiatrists showed too much consensus about the categories
(c) Pinel's therapy was more effective
(d) mental illness is really caused by evil spirits

Somatic therapies

7. Early approaches to somatic therapy may have seemed to work because of the _____ the patients were getting

8. The three main types of somatic intervention are chemical, physical and _____

9. Treating psychiatric disorders with drugs is known as _____

The medical model

10. Patients may adopt the idea of "mental illness" because it frees them from being _____ for their condition

11. Szasz thought that it was better to look at problems in _____ than mental illness

12. One problem with the idea of abnormal behaviour as mental illness is that:
(a) it involves somatic therapy
(b) it always identifies organic origins
(c) it locates the problem in the individual not in society
(d) it avoids making judgements about people

DSM-IIIR

13. Axis 5 of DSM-IIIR involves:
(a) clinical syndromes
(b) highest level of adaptive functioning during the year
(c) physical disorders
(d) psychosocial stressors

14. DSM-IIIR was designed to address problems of low _____ in psychiatric diagnosis

15. DSM-IIIR is an improvement on Kraepelin's system because it takes into account _____ and personal factors

Normality & abnormality

16. Which of the following were not identified as criteria for abnormal behaviour by Rosenhan and Seligman:
(a) violation of moral standards
(b) vividness and unconventionality
(c) unpredictability
(d) artistic genius

17. The difference between normal and abnormal behaviour is elusive because:
(a) not everyone experiences symptoms
(b) the symptoms are too vague to be applied
(c) everyone experiences symptoms to some degree
(d) no-one experiences extremes of the symptoms

18. Jahoda's criterion that people should be able to act independently and make their own reasoned judgements is known as _____

Schizophrenia

19. A schizophrenic is a person suffering from:
(a) split personality
(b) low intelligence
(c) separation from reality
(d) cyclical manic-depression

20. Which of the following is not known to be a factor in schizophrenia:
(a) genetic influences
(b) lack of exercise
(c) family influence
(d) brain chemistry

21. Bateson et al. identified the
_____ as a factor in schizophrenia

Depression

22. Oscillating between periods of
depression and periods of elation is known
as _____ depression

23. Seligman compared the apathy of
clinical depression with _____ in
animals

24. Having a biological predisposition to
depression means that a person will:
(a) definitely develop depression
(b) definitely not develop depression
(c) never pass depression on to their
children
(d) be less able to overcome the effects of
stress

Eating disorders

25. The two main types of anorexia are
nervosa and _____

26. The idea that anorexia has a
physiological cause was criticised because
it ignored:
(a) social factors
(b) psychological factors
(c) nutritional factors
(d) health factors

27. The _____ explanation of
anorexia is that fatness and pregnancy are
perceived as the same thing

REVISION QUESTIONS

1. *Describe the five early categories of mental illness*

2. *What are the axes of DSM-IIIR?*

3. *Outline the cognitive approach to depression*

ESSAY QUESTIONS

1. *Discuss some of the problems of psychiatric diagnosis. To what extent can the system of diagnosis represented by DSM-IIIR overcome these problems?*

2. *Is "problems in living" a more useful concept than "mental illness"? Give reasons for your answer*

3. *Is schizophrenia inherited?*

USEFUL FURTHER READING

Rosenhan, D. L. & Seligman, M. E. P. (1989) *Abnormal psychology* (2nd ed.) London: W. W. Norton & Co.

Bootzin, R. R., Acocella, J. R., & Alloy, L. B. (1993) *Abnormal psychology: current perspectives* (6th ed.) New York: McGraw Hill

McKellar, P. (1989) *Abnormal psychology: its experience and behaviour* London: Routledge

CHAPTER 9   ALTERNATIVES TO THE MEDICAL MODEL

The key issues

This chapter addresses some of the major approaches to therapy which have been proposed as alternatives to the medical model. It begins by looking at the three major, and very different, alternatives put forward by the psychoanalytic, behaviourist, and humanistic schools of thought in psychology. Each of these different models is described, together with its implications for therapy.

The chapter then goes on to look at some of the more specific approaches to understanding abnormal behaviour. It begins by exploring Laing's existentialist approach, before going on to consider the more cognitive approaches put forward by Aaron Back and the personal construct psychologists. Finally, the chapter examines some of the more specific approaches to therapy: rational-emotive therapy, Gestalt therapy, transactional analysis, and family therapy.

Chapter summary

1. Psychoanalysis is a form of therapy which was initially developed on the basis of Freud's model of personality, although other forms developed subsequently. Critics of psychoanalysis have argued that it has little effect, despite being extremely widespread and influential.

2. Behaviour therapy was developed through applying learning theory to problems of abnormal behaviour. Behaviour therapy techniques can be seen as those based on classical conditioning, those based on operant conditioning, and those based on social learning.

3. Client-centred therapy is based on Rogers' theory of personality, and takes the view that if the individual is given unconditional positive regard, they will be able to sort out their own personal problems.

4. Existentialist therapy sees people as having chosen their own actions, including retreat into illness. It emphasises the context within which the person exists, and how they respond to the demands on them. Its emphasis on family interactions in schizophrenia led to the eventual development of family therapy.

5. Cognitive therapy aims to identify distorted cognitions, so that the person can understand their situation more positively and act to change it. It focusses on expectations, appraisals, attributions and beliefs.

6. Personal construct therapy is based on the idea that everyone has their own, unique way of construing the world. Therapy aims to encourage people to change their personal construct system so as to understand events in a more positive way.

7. Rational-emotive therapy aims to counteract irrational and self-defeating beliefs, partly through logical argument and partly through re-training the person to feel comfortable with other ideas.

8. Gestalt therapy emphasises the whole cognitive field, or gestalt, within which an experience takes place, and encourages people to develop greater awareness of the active Gestalts which they are operating at any given moment.

9. Transactional analysis interprets social interaction in terms of Games, which can often help people to perceive patterns in their interaction with others and so change it.

10. Family therapy emphasises the person within their family context. Object relations therapists emphasise past events within the family, while systems therapists construe the family as a current working system. Structural family therapy emphasises boundaries and divisions within the family, while strategic intervention therapy adopts a problem-centred approach.

LEARNING OBJECTIVES

1. **Psychoanalysis**
   The student shall be able to:
   - describe the process of psychoanalysis
   - define key terms in psychoanalysis
   - list Eysenck's criticisms of psychoanalysis

2. **Behaviour therapy**
   The student shall be able to:
   - describe techniques of behaviour therapy
   - explain the learning principles underlying behaviour therapies
   - evaluate behaviourist explanations of behaviour therapy

3. **Client-centred therapy**
   The student shall be able to:
   - define Rogers' concept of psychological health
   - outline the origins of mental disorders in Rogers' theory
   - describe the central features of client-centred therapy

4. **Existentialist therapy**
   The student shall be able to:
   - define terms relating to existentialist therapy
   - list the characteristics of a double-bind
   - describe the existentialist explanation for schizophrenia

5. **Cognitive therapy**
   The student shall be able to:
   - outline the four central aspects of cognitive therapy
   - identify different types of attributions
   - list the dimensions of the Leeds Attributional Coding System

6. **PCT & RET**
   The student shall be able to:
   - distinguish between tight and loose construct systems
   - identify types of unrealistic ideas challenged in RET
   - describe methods for inducing personal change in PCT & RET

7. **Gestalt therapy and transactional analysis**
   The student shall be able to:
   - describe basic concepts in Gestalt therapy
   - define terms relating to transactional analysis
   - identify therapeutic techniques used in Gestalt therapy & TA

8. Family therapy

The student shall be able to:
- define terms relating to family therapy
- outline the four major approaches to family therapy
- describe concepts of family disturbance and intervention

OBJECTIVE QUESTIONS

Psychoanalysis

1. Psychoanalysis explains mental disorders in terms of unconscious inner

_____

2. Defence mechanisms are used to:
(a) protect from psychological threat
(b) defend against physical danger
(c) prevent social disturbances
(d) avoid lying

3. Which of the following was not one of Eysenck's criticisms of psychoanalysis:
(a) people having psychoanalysis improved at the same rate as people without treatment
(b) psychoanalysis didn't make any difference whether soldiers would return to duty or not
(c) recovery under psychoanalysis is no quicker than recovery under eclectic therapy
(d) There is no difference between males and females in responses to psychoanalysis

Behaviour therapy

4. Systematic desensitisation is a way of:
(a) gradually reducing a phobia
(b) applying ECT
(c) avoiding punishment
(d) rapidly reducing a phobia

5. Implosion therapy is based on the principle of _____

6. Behaviourist explanations of behaviour therapy were criticised because they ignored:
(a) overt behaviour
(b) the relationship with the therapist
(c) the importance of the stimulus
(d) the importance of the response

Client-centred therapy

7. Rogers believed that psychologically healthy people achieve positive regard and _____

8. Rogers believed that anxiety stemmed from:
(a) the rift between inner and outer self
(b) the split between ideal and actual self
(c) self-actualisation
(d) ontological insecurity

9. Rogers argued that client-centred therapists must be empathic, genuine and _____

Existentialist therapy

10. Laing believed that ontologically _____ individuals have experienced dysfunctional families

11. Which of the following is not a necessary ingredient of a double-bind:
(a) repeated exposure
(b) a secondary positive injunction
(c) a primary negative injunction
(d) two or more persons

12. Laing believed that schizophrenia is an existential _____ made by the individual

Cognitive therapy

13. How a person evaluates a situation or event is known as an _____

14. Claiming that exams depend on luck is making a _____ attribution

15. Which of the following is not a dimension of the LACS:
(a) global / specific
(b) stable / unstable
(c) positive / negative
(d) controllable / uncontrollable

PCT & RET

16. An inflexible construct system is referred to as a _____ system

17. Unrealistic ideas challenged in rational-emotive therapy do not include:
(a) other people must always be rational
(b) the world should always be a fair and unfrustrating place
(c) you must always like everyone else
(d) you should never succeed

18. The most important aspect of rational-emotive therapy is the cognitive _____ that the client has to do

Other   therapies

19. The central concept in Gestalt therapy is that of _____

20. In TA, a _____ is a unit of human communication

21. One Gestalt technique involves:
(a) challenging irrational beliefs
(b) identifying parent, adult and child states
(c) getting to know an orange
(d) deliberately breaking an appointment

Family   therapy

22. When disturbed families insist on a façade of family harmony, this is known as _____

23. Strategic intervention therapy concentrates on:
(a) solving the immediate presenting problem
(b) the family as a working system
(c) coming to terms with the past
(d) the divisions which occur in the family

24. Which of the following is not a technique used in family therapy:
(a) seeing several families together
(b) charting the family system
(c) re-enacting crucial family events
(d) refusing to see members of the family

REVISION QUESTIONS

1. *Briefly outline the assumptions and ideas in the existentialist approach to therapy*

2. *Describe the main types of cognition addressed by cognitive therapists*

3. *Outline the basic principles of either Gestalt or rational-emotive therapy*

ESSAY QUESTIONS

1. *What are the advantages and disadvantages of psychoanalysis?*

2. *"Where behaviour therapy works, it does so for entirely different reasons than those assumed by the behaviourists". Discuss, with reference to specific forms of behaviour therapy*

3. *Compare and contrast client-centred therapy and personal construct therapy*

USEFUL FURTHER READING

Fonagy, P. & Higgitt, A. (1984) *Personality theory and clinical practice* London: Methuen

Rogers, C. R. (1961) *On becoming a person: a therapist's view of psychotherapy* London: Constable

Eysenck, H. J. (1985) *The decline and fall of the Freudian empire* Harmondsworth: Penguin

CHAPTER 10   SENSATION AND BRAIN MECHANISMS

The key issues

In this chapter, we are looking at the central and peripheral nervous systems, and at how they process incoming information. The chapter begins by exploring how sensory information, in its several different forms, is received and transduced into electrical impulses. It then goes on to look at the processing of visual information in more detail, before identifying the three major types of nerve cells incorporated in the reflex arc, and how they work together to produce co-ordinated action.

The second part of the chapter is concerned with the processing of more complex information in the cerebrum. It begins with an exploration of the methods involved in studying brain functioning, before going on to consider some of the non-localised functions of the cerebral cortex. The chapter then goes on to describe the specific areas involved in language processing and production, before looking at issues of hemisphere differences raised by split-brain experiments and other methods of investigation.

Chapter summary

1. The peripheral nervous system consists of sensory receptors, which transduce sensation into electrical impulses, and neurones which transmit those messages to the central nervous system. Different senses have receptors responsive to different types of information.

2. Sensory information is processed and decoded in the central nervous system. Both the thalamus and the visual cortex of the cerebrum are involved in decoding visual information.

3. The reflex arc is a simple representation of the action of the three main types of neurone: sensory neurones, connector neurones, and motor neurones. These convey electrical impulses generated by electro-chemical interactions.

4. Methods of studying the brain include physical interventions, such as lesion and ablation; chemical injection, electrical interventions such as micro-electrode recording, EEGs, and evoked potential recordings, and scanning techniques.

5. Clinical neuropsychology is the study of how the brain functions. Studies of personality, learning and memory indicate that these cannot be specifically localised in one part of the brain.

6. Studies of language functioning show that there are three distinct language processing areas in the brain: Broca's area, Wernicke's area, and the angular gyrus. These are generally located on the left hemisphere.

7. Studies of hemisphere functioning have shown that motor and sensory functions are located on the opposite cerebral hemisphere from the relevant side of the body. In terms of hemisphere dominance, however, there seems to be only a slight relationship between language and handedness.

8. Split-brain studies and other research indicates that spatial and analytical functions tend to be located in different hemispheres, although there can be some crossover of function between the two.

LEARNING OBJECTIVES

1. **The nervous system**
    The student shall be able to:
    - define terms relating to the nervous system
    - describe the three parts of the nervous system
    - link parts of the nervous system with everyday experience

2. **Sensory information processing**
    The student shall be able to:
    - identify the major receptors for different senses
    - link physiological factors in sensation with experience
    - describe the processing of visual information

3. **The reflex arc**
    The student shall be able to:
    - describe the structures of neurones which comprise the reflex arc
    - outline the passage of neural information in the reflex arc
    - explain the concepts of summation and habituation

4. **Methods of studying the brain**
    The student shall be able to:
    - describe methods of studying brain functioning
    - identify limitations of different methods of studying the brain
    - evaluate the use of animals in studying brain functioning

5. **Clinical neuropsychology**
    The student shall be able to:
    - define key terms relating to clinical neuropsychology
    - link disturbances in brain function with memory disorders
    - evaluate the relationship between brain function and
      personality

6. **Language functions**
    The student shall be able to:
    - identify areas of the cerebrum involved in language
    - describe language disorders resulting from cerebral damage
    - apply knowledge of brain functioning to everyday experience

7. **Hemisphere differences**
    The student shall be able to:
    - define terms relating to hemisphere differences
    - describe a study of hemisphere differences
    - apply knowledge of hemisphere function to everyday experience

8. **Spatial and analytical functions**
    The student shall be able to:
    - describe Sperry's studies of people with split brains
    - evaluate approaches to understanding hemisphere differences
    - discuss the relationship between hemisphere differences and
      creativity

OBJECTIVE QUESTIONS

The nervous system

1. The nervous system consists of millions of cells called:
(a) neurotics
(b) neurones
(c) neurotransmitters
(d) neuroplasms

2. The central nervous system consists of the _____ and spinal cord

3. The part of the nervous system involved in feelings of emotion is the _____ nervous system

Sensory information

4. Rod cells are used for:
(a) hearing
(b) seeing
(c) tasting
(d) smelling

5. Amputation often produces _____ limbs

6. The optic nerve synapses in the

_____

The reflex arc

7. Nerve cells which carry information from the sense receptors to the CNS are known as _____ neurones

8. Place the following consequences of putting the hand on a hot iron in order:
(a) connector neurone passes message to motor neurone
(b) motor neurone tells muscle to contract
(c) sensory information reaches spinal cord
(d) sensory neurone is stimulated

9. Habituation is:
(a) responding to a stimulus over and over again
(b) ceasing to register an incoming stimulus
(c) continually registering incoming information
(d) always repeating the same action

Methods of studying

10. Ablation is:
(a) the surgical removal of part of the brain
(b) damage to part of the brain
(c) putting electrodes into cells of the brain
(d) using radioactive labelling to study the brain

11. It is difficult to study consequences of accidental brain injury because:
(a) people don't socialise after brain damage
(b) researchers do not know people with brain injury
(c) prior problems may be attributed to the injury
(d) other people avoid those with brain damage

12. Gray showed how animal experiments had led to improved _____ drugs

Clinical neuropsychology

13. Leucotomy involves:
(a) removing the frontal lobe of the brain
(b) stimulating the frontal lobe of the brain electrically
(c) injecting chemicals into the frontal lobe of the brain
(d) severing connections between the frontal lobe and the rest of the brain

14. ECT can cause _____ amnesia

15. One problem in the use of frontal lobotomy for psychiatric patients was the lack of _____ studies

Language functions

16. The area of the cerebrum associated with reading is the _____

17. Wernicke described a syndrome in which patients:
(a) had problems speaking
(b) had problems hearing what was said to them
(c) had problems understanding what was said to them
(d) had problems with reading

18. Put these parts of the brain in order to describe the process of reading aloud
(a) Broca's area
(b) the angular gyrus
(c) the motor cortex
(d) Wernicke's area

Hemisphere differences

19. Illustrations of how motor and sensory areas of the brain influence the body produce:
(a) synaptic clefts
(b) homunculi
(c) histograms
(d) logogens

20. Penfield and Rasmussen used _____ stimulation to study areas of the cerebrum

21. Problems moving the right arm after a stroke show that the _____ hemisphere has been damaged

Spatial functions

22. Sperry found that split-brain patients could only say words presented in the _____ visual field

23. One of the problems with evidence from split-brain studies is that:
(a) it comes from people with abnormal brains
(b) the results are difficult to interpret
(c) all parts of the brain are equipotential
(d) it is inconclusive

24. Trained musicians seem to use the _____ hemisphere to process musical information

REVISION QUESTIONS

1. *Briefly outline how visual information is processed*

2. *What is the reflex arc, and what types of neurones does it involve?*

3. *What are the main areas for language processing in the brain, and what do they do?*

ESSAY QUESTIONS

1. *Giving examples, critically evaluate the main methods of studying brain functioning*

2. *To what extent are the functions of the cerebrum localised?*

3. *To what extent can behaviour be explained in terms of the activity of the nervous system?*

USEFUL FURTHER READING

Beaumont, J. G. (1991) *Understanding neuropsychology* Oxford: Blackwell

Carlson, N. R. (1992) *Foundations of physiological psychology* (2nd ed.) London: Allyn & Bacon

Rose, S. (1992) *The making of memory* London: Bantam Press

CHAPTER 11   SLEEP, DREAMING AND CONSCIOUSNESS

The key issues

This chapter is concerned with the relationship between physiology, social experience, and the various kinds of states of consciousness which are experienced by human beings. It begins by looking at circadian rhythms, and how these can influence how effectively people process information and respond to different tasks or situations. It then looks at the different states of sleep, and at the different parts of the central nervous system which appear to be involved in states of sleeping and wakefulness, before going on to consider theories of dreaming.

The chapter then moves on to consider different types of psychoactive drugs, and the way that some of these drugs influence neural functioning by affecting the actions of neurotransmitters at the synapse. It then looks at the altered state of consciousness which we know as hypnosis, particularly addressing the issue of whether hypnosis has to be regarded as a special state, or whether hypnotic phenomena can be explained in terms of more conventional psychological mechanisms.

Chapter summary

1. The body has many natural rhythms, including circadian rhythms, which incorporate alternating periods of sleeping and waking. These are strongly influenced by external zeitgebers.

2. While we are asleep, we alternate between periods of quiet sleep, which appears to be concerned with tissue restoration, and active sleep, during which we make rapid eye movements and are more likely to dream.

3. Some of the more important physiological structures involved in sleep are the locus coeruleus and the raphé nuclei of the reticular activating system. These have links with other areas of the brain, and involve the neurotransmitters serotonin and noradrenaline.

4. Theories of dreaming include the idea that dreaming is disguised unconscious wish-fulfilment, that it is simply a by-product of neural activity, and that it allows the brain to sort out new information and link it with prior knowledge.

5. Methods of studying consciousness have included studies of neural activity, sensory deprivation, brain surgery, and psychoactive drugs.

6. Psychoactive drugs are those which directly affect the mind, by influencing the actions of neurotransmitters at the synapse. These include sedatives and depressants, stimulants, opiates and narcotics, and hallucinogens. Recreational drugs, whether legal or illegal, tend to be psychoactive.

7. State theorists of hypnotism see it as a special state of consciousness, allowing access to parts of the mind which are otherwise inaccessible.

8. Non-state theorists of hypnotism see it as a social phenomenon, which can be explained in terms of well-known social psychological mechanisms.

LEARNING OBJECTIVES

1.   **Biological rhythms**
     The student shall be able to:
     - identify features of human circadian rhythms
     - apply knowledge of human circadian rhythms to shift work
     - link human circadian rhythms with everyday life

2. **Types of sleep**
   The student shall be able to:
   - define terms relating to different types of sleep
   - describe features of sleep cycles
   - distinguish between explanations for sleep cycles

3. **Physiology of sleep**
   The student shall be able to:
   - identify major physiological structures involved in sleep
   - describe a study of sleep processes
   - outline the major effects of sleep deprivation or restriction

4. **Theories of dreaming**
   The student shall be able to:
   - describe a study of dreaming
   - outline major theories of dreaming
   - evaluate theories of dreaming

5. **Studying consciousness**
   The student shall be able to:
   - define terms relating to the study of consciousness
   - describe methods of studying consciousness
   - evaluate methods of studying consciousness

6. **Drugs and neurotransmitters**
   The student shall be able to:
   - describe the functions of the synapse
   - outline the types of psychoactive drugs
   - show how drugs may affect consciousness

7. **State approaches to hypnotism**
   The student shall be able to:
   - identify types of hypnotic phenomena
   - describe Hilgard's model of hypnosis
   - evaluate evidence for hypnosis as a special state

8. **Social theories of hypnotism**
   The student shall be able to:
   - define terms relating to the psychological study of hypnotism
   - identify social mechanisms contributing to hypnotic experience
   - apply social explanations to hypnotic phenomena

OBJECTIVE QUESTIONS

Biological rhythms

1. External events which affect circadian rhythms are known as _____

2. Which of the following sequences of shifts would be preferable:
(a) night, afternoon, morning
(b) morning, night, afternoon
(c) morning, afternoon, night
(d) a random mixture of shifts during the week

3. The most practical remedy for tired drivers is to:
(a) stop and have something to eat
(b) pull over and sleep
(c) play music and sing loudly
(d) drink lots of black coffee

Types of sleep

4. REM stands for:
(a) revolving eye movements
(b) rapid eye monitoring
(c) rapid eye mechanism
(d) rapid eye movement

5. We are hardest to wake up when we are in level _____ sleep

6. Meddis argued that active sleep evolved _____ quiet sleep

Physiology of sleep

7. The pineal gland secretes _____ , which produces drowsiness

8. Moruzzi and Magoun used _____ to measure activity in the RAS

9. Prolonged sleep deprivation:
(a) affects short-term tasks but not repetitive ones
(b) affects repetitive tasks but not short-term ones
(c) makes the person jumpy and nervous
(d) makes us unable to react to alarming stimuli

Theories of dreaming

10. Dement and Kleitman studied the content of dreaming by:
(a) giving a signal when someone began REM sleep
(b) spending several days and nights in a large cave
(c) investigating the meaning of dreamwork symbols
(d) spraying water on people in REM sleep

11. Evan saw dreaming as a process which:
(a) helps us to make sense out of information
(b) helps us to forget our experiences
(c) acts as unconscious wish-fulfilment
(d) allows the brain to rest

12. Which of the following is not a criticism which has been made of Freud's theory of dreaming:
(a) it is scientifically untestable
(b) Freud was not a dream analyst
(c) it may rest on over-interpreting the evidence
(d) the analysis of dreams is retrospective

Studying consciousness

13. A measure of overall brain activity is known as an _____

14. Sensory deprivation involves:
(a) being blindfolded
(b) being blindfolded and floating in water
(c) putting on ear pads
(d) all of the above

15. Penfield used electrical _____ as a way of studying the brain

Drugs

16. The _____ is the place where electrical impulses are passed from one neurone to another

17. Amphetamine is a _____ drug

18. Hallucinogenic drugs:
(a) produce a placebo effect
(b) enhance sleep patterns
(c) put people into hypnotic states
(d) enhance or distort perception

State hypnotism

19. Hypnotism is useful in helping people to control and reduce _____

20. Hilgard referred to the aware part of the person during hypnosis as the

_____

21. The idea of hypnosis as a special state has been criticised because:
(a) some people can't be hypnotised
(b) there is a "hidden observer"
(c) it can equally be explained by other social mechanisms
(d) some people have lived before

Social hypnotism

22. Hypnotising yourself is known as
_____

23. Which of the following has not been used to explain hypnotism:
(a) social identity
(b) social roles and expectations
(c) demand characteristics of the situation
(d) conformity

24. Hypnotic _____ can be shown to involve information which people have already learned about, even if they don't always remember doing so

REVISION QUESTIONS

1. *Describe the physiological processes involved in the experience of jet lag*

2. *Outline the different types of sleep, and their physiological characteristics*

3. *What are the main methods which have been used to study consciousness?*

ESSAY QUESTIONS

1. *Critically evaluate experimental evidence for, and theories of, dreaming*

2. *How far can the actions of drugs be understood in terms of physiological brain processes?*

3. *Is hypnosis a special state of awareness?*

USEFUL FURTHER READING

Green, S. (1987) *Physiological psychology: an introduction* London: Routledge & Kegan Paul

Kalat, James W. (1992) *Biological psychology* (4th ed.) London: Thompson International Publishing

Plant, M. (1987) *Drugs in perspective* London: Hodder & Stoughton

CHAPTER 12   MOTIVATION AND EMOTION

The key issues
The first half of this chapter is concerned with the different types of motivation experienced by human beings. As such, it begins by exploring the basic, physiological states of motivation such as hunger and thirst, along with their physiological implications, but then ranges more broadly, to include more complex and socially-oriented forms of motivation such as the need for positive regard or social respect.

In its second part, the chapter addressses the question of emotion, taking a similarly broad perspective ranging from physiological to social dimensions. It begins by examining the concept of arousal, and looking at the various theories which have been put forward to explain negative emotions, and concludes by looking at some of the research into more positive emotions which has been undertaken by psychologists.

Chapter summary

1. Drive theories of motivation were popular in the first half of the century. They saw motivation as arising from internal needs, producing drives. A popular distinction was between primary drives, satisfying basic physiological needs, and secondary drives, which were more wide-ranging and sometimes cognitive.

2. Physiological studies of hunger identified two areas of the hypothalamus, one concerned with feeding and the other with satiation. These have been linked with neurotransmitter activity, and with the concept of a neurological set-weight for the body.

3. Exploration is a complex form of motivation which may link with some brain activities, but is also strongly influenced by environmental factors. Studies of direct electrical brain stimulation led to a distinction between incentives and rewards in motivation.

4. Theories of human motivation have identified several psychological needs, including needs for achievement, for positive social regard, for self-actualisation, for respect from others, and for control over the effects of one's actions.

5. The arousal response results from the action of the sympathetic nervous system and the endocrine system. Studies of arousal resulted in the Yerkes-Dodson law of performance and arousal, and some debate about the usefulness of arousal as a generalised concept.

6. Selye identified a general adaptation response to long-term stress, which could produce gastric problems and lowered resistance to illness. Long-term stress has also been linked to locus of control, and to type A and B behaviour patterns.

7. "Classic" theories of emotion include the James-Lange theory of emotion, the Cannon-Bard theory of emotion, and Schachter and Singer's model. Later theories of emotion include appraisal theory, attribution theory, the facial feedback theory, and the theory of emotion as transitory social roles.

8. Research into positive emotions has identified the four dimensions of absorption, potency, altruism and spiritual experience. Other research into positive emotions includes investigation of the social emotion of humour, and the complex emotion of love.

LEARNING OBJECTIVES

1. **Drive theories**
    The student shall be able to:
    - define terms relating to drive theories of motivation
    - describe processes relating to maintaining homeostasis
    - identify limitations of drive theories of motivation

2. **Hunger**
   The student shall be able to:
   - name physiological mechanisms involved in hunger
   - describe a study of hunger
   - outline evidence for a biological set-weight regulating hunger

3. **Exploration and incentives**
   The student shall be able to:
   - identify implications of studies of exploration
   - describe a study of electrical stimulation of the brain
   - distinguish between incentives and rewards

4. **Human motives**
   The student shall be able to:
   - describe a study of achievement motivation
   - evaluate Maslow's theory of human needs
   - describe the human needs identified by Rogers and Harré

5. **Arousal**
   The student shall be able to:
   - describe methods of studying arousal
   - outline the Yerkes-Dodson Law of arousal
   - evaluate the concept of general arousal

6. **Stress**
   The student shall be able to:
   - identify effects of long-term stress
   - describe a study of long-term stress
   - describe therapies for reducing long-term stress

7. **Theories of emotion**
   The student shall be able to:
   - distinguish between early theories
   - describe a study of emotion
   - identify theories of emotion

8. **Positive emotions**
   The student shall be able to:
   - identify the major functions of humour
   - name different types of loving
   - describe the four dimensions of positive emotions

Drive theories

1. The term which means maintaining a steady physiological state is:
(a) homeopathic
(b) homo sapiens
(c) homophonic
(d) homeostasis

2. Drives which have been acquired through learning are known as _____ drives

3. Rogers argued that the need for self-_____ could not be explained by drive theory

Hunger

4. The brain structure known as the _____ is involved in regulating hunger

5. Anand and Brobeck showed that a lesion in the lateral hypothalamus would cause animals to:
(a) eat only selected foods
(b) overeat and become obese
(c) starve themselves
(d) vomit their food

6. Schachter found that _____ people would eat more at a sitting but were finicky about their food

7. Welker proposed that _____ in rats is linked with the motivation to escape

8. Gallistel showed that learning using ESB as a reward would _____ very quickly

9. Which of the following best describes an incentive:
(a) encourages behaviour and reduces drives
(b) encourages behaviour and doesn't reduce drives
(c) reduces internal drives
(d) increases internal drives

10. Which of the following methods was not used by McClelland to study achievement motivation:
(a) asking children to build a tower blindfolded
(b) looking at literature in different countries
(c) asking children to complete a story
(d) looking at teachers' reports of children

11. Maslow's theory cannot explain the behaviour of anorexics, who fulfil social needs before _____ ones

12. Harré argued that social _____ is a fundamental motivator for human beings

13. The GSR is a measure of:
(a) how hot the skin is
(b) how active the person is
(c) how pale the skin is
(d) how much the person is sweating

14. The Yerkes-Dodson Law states that:
(a) the more arousal, the better the performance
(b) the less arousal, the better the performance
(c) arousal improves performance only up to a point, then decreases it
(d) arousal decreases performance only up to a point, then improves it

15. The idea of general arousal has been criticised because:
(a) there are several different types of arousal
(b) arousal is difficult to measure
(c) arousal doesn't really happen
(d) people also become aroused through exercise

Stress

16. The second stage of long-term stress, according to Selye, is the _____ stage

17. Brady used _____ to study the effects of stressful activity

18. _____ is used to inform people of their physiological state so that they can learn to relax

Emotion

19. Which of the following best describes the James-Lange theory of emotion:
(a) emotion is followed by physiological reaction
(b) physiological changes produce emotional changes
(c) physiological and emotional changes are independent of one another
(d) physiological and emotional changes occur simultaneously

20. Marañon studied emotion by:
(a) injecting people with adrenaline
(b) showing men pictures of nude women
(c) tripping up on the stairs
(d) using stooges to simulate moods

21. Ekman proposed the _____ feedback theory of emotion

Positive emotions

22. Which of the following was not identified by Kuhn as a primary function of humour:
(a) expressing hostility
(b) communication
(c) constructing reality
(d) coping

23. Tennov distinguished between love and _____

24. The dimension of positive emotion which describes the amount of concentration which an activity demands is:
(a) altruism
(b) potency
(c) spiritual
(d) absorption

REVISION QUESTIONS

1. *Giving examples, briefly describe the concept of homeostasis*

2. *How do studies of exploration challenge drive-reduction theories of motivation?*

3. *Identify sources of individual difference which can make people more or less susceptible to stress*

ESSAY QUESTIONS

1. *What can a knowledge of physiological mechanisms tell us about human motivation?*

2. *Describe physiological and alternative explanations of the experience of emotion*

3. *Compare and contrast psychological research into negative and positive emotions*

USEFUL FURTHER READING

Evans, P. (1989) *Motivation and emotion* London: Routledge

Cox, T. (1989) *Stress* (2nd ed.) London: Routledge

Argyle, M. (1991) *The psychology of happiness* Harmondsworth: Penguin

CHAPTER 13   SELF AND OTHERS

The key issues

This chapter is concerned with the way that individual human beings relate to the others around them. It begins by examining the idea of the self-concept, and the social implications which are contained in ideas about the individual self, before examining other dimensions of self such as social identifications and cross-cultural perspectives.

The chapter then goes on to consider psychological research into attraction and dating behaviour, including recent critiques of this research as being relatively superficial and ethnocentric. It then attempts to develop a deeper perspective on these issues through a consideration of research into relationship development, maintenance and breakdown, and the experience of loneliness.

Chapter summary

1. Feedback from others, social interaction, the maintenance of self-esteem, self-perception and self-efficacy beliefs are significant factors in the maintenance of the self-concept.

2. Social identity theory argues that the social groups to which the individual belongs are important in how we see ourselves and how we interact with others.

3. The Western concept of the self as an isolated, independent entity is not one which is shared by most human cultures. Instead, the self is more likely to be seen as embedded within a social and cultural network.

4. Factors influencing interpersonal attraction include physical attractiveness, similarity and complementarity, familiarity and propinquity, reciprocal liking, and perceived fallibility. Theoretical explanations of attraction have included evaluation, social reinforcement, and cognitive similarity.

5. Early theories of relationships tended to use economic metaphors, such as applying social exchange or equity theory. Later theories tended to emphasise cognitive similarity and the way that relationships change over time.

6. Studies of relationship development have looked at how self-presentation, non-verbal communication, and self-disclosure are managed in the early stages of relationships. Studies of relationship maintenance have emphasised reciprocal obligations, and providing social support.

7. Relationships may break down as a result of breaking the rules, lack of stimulation, or unmet expectations. Duck identified four phases of relationship breakdown: the intra-psychic phase, the dyadic phase, the social phase, and the grave-dressing phase.

8. Studies of loneliness have shown that chronically lonely people may interact differently with others, using less self-disclosure and giving partners less attention. They also tend to see interpersonal situations as less easily influenced.

LEARNING OBJECTIVES

1. **Self-concept**
    The student shall be able to:
    - define terms relating to processes of the self-concept
    - identify mechanisms contributing to the self-concept
    - describe a study of the self-concept

2. **Social identification**
   The student shall be able to:
   - describe the basic processes of social identification
   - evaluate methods of studying social identification
   - apply concepts of social identification to everyday life

3. **Cultural concepts of self**
   The student shall be able to:
   - identify social and cultural influences on the self-concept
   - distinguish between different cultural conceptions of self
   - evaluate the idea of the independent self-concept

4. **Interpersonal attraction**
   The student shall be able to:
   - describe factors influencing attraction
   - identify theories of attraction
   - evaluate the psychological study of attraction

5. **Theories of relationships**
   The student shall be able to:
   - define terms relating to the study of relationships
   - describe theories of relationships
   - identify problematic assumptions in early studies of
     relationships

6. **Relationship processes**
   The student shall be able to:
   - list Hinde's dimensions for studying relationships
   - identify interpersonal processes in development of relationships
   - describe strategies of relationship maintenance

7. **Relationship breakdown**
   The student shall be able to:
   - list rules and expectations about relationships and friendships
   - identify reasons for relationship breakdown
   - describe Duck's four stages of relationship breakdown

8. **Loneliness**
   The student shall be able to:
   - distinguish beween situational and chronic loneliness
   - identify social differences between lonely and non-lonely people
   - describe cognitive aspects of loneliness

OBJECTIVE QUESTIONS

Self-concept

1. The evaluative component of the self-concept is known as _____

2. Self-efficacy refers to beliefs about our own perceived:
(a) body-image
(b) self-worth
(c) competences
(d) attitudes

3. Coopersmith found that high self-esteem correlates positively with _____ expectations

Social identification

4. Social identity theory proposes that we sometimes interact with people as _____ of our social groups

5. One problem with minimal group studies is that people respond to:
(a) limited abilities
(b) other people's views
(c) which team is best
(d) demand characteristics

6. People who leave a job because they feel that it is too low-status are showing:
(a) social representations
(b) negative social identification
(c) categorisation
(d) self-efficacy

Cultural concepts

7. DeVos argued that _____ people are particularly sensitive to interpersonal guilt

8. According to Nobles, European thought is based on "control over nature", whereas traditional African thought is based on being " _____ with nature"

9. One problem of the idea of the independent self is that it ignores:
(a) social contexts
(b) emotional feelings
(c) individual needs
(d) parental influences

Interpersonal attraction

10. Propinquity means _____ closeness

11. The theory that we like people who think like us is known as:
(a) reciprocal liking
(b) attraction as evaluation
(c) attraction as cognitive similarity
(d) attraction as reinforcement

12. An alternative explanation for equal attractiveness in partners is fear of _____

Relationships

13. The theory that relationships involve bargaining for the best deal is _____ theory

14. The idea that relationships have to be evenly balanced is known as:
(a) balance theory
(b) equity theory
(c) reinforcement theory
(d) reciprocal theory

15. Early theories of relationships were problematic because they approached relationships as:
(a) dynamic
(b) static
(c) circular
(d) spirals

Relationship processes

16. The dimension describing the number and range of activities in a relationship is

_____

17. Self-disclosure is:
(a) telling people about ourselves
(b) finding out about ourselves
(c) looking at our own motives
(d) hiding our real opinions

18. According to Ayer, which of the following is not a strategy for maintaining relationships:
(a) balance
(b) directness
(c) avoidance
(d) reminiscing

Relationship breakdown

19. Friendship involves reciprocal
_____ between the two people

20. Duck and Miell identified lack of
_____ as a reason for relationship
breakdown

21. The phase in which someone decides
privately that they are justified in
leaving a relationship is the:
(a) grave-dressing phase
(b) dyadic phase
(c) intra-psychic phase
(d) social phase

Loneliness

22. Temporary loneliness is described as
situational, but ongoing loneliness is
described as _____

23. Lonely people give their partners less
_____ than non-lonely people

24. Cognitive aspects of loneliness involve:
(a) limerence
(b) dispositions
(c) attributions
(d) apathy

REVISION QUESTIONS

1. *Briefly outline the main factors in the maintenance of the self-concept*

2. *Describe the major factors influencing interpersonal attraction*

3. *Outline the four phases of relationship breakdown*

ESSAY QUESTIONS

1. *"The concept of the independent individual is a delusion". Discuss.*

2. *Critically evaluate psychological theories of attraction*

3. *"Studying relationships is more useful to understanding human beings than studying attraction". Discuss*

USEFUL FURTHER READING

Marsella, A. J., DeVos, G., & Hsu, F. L. K. (1985) *Culture and self: Asian and Western perspectives* London: Tavistock/Methuen

Hinde, R. A. (1987) *Individuals, relationships and culture* Cambridge: Cambridge University Press

Duck, S. (1988) *Relating to others* Milton Keynes: Open University Press

CHAPTER 14   UNDERSTANDING OTHERS

The key issues

This chapter is concerned primarily with how we come to understand other people. It begins by looking at various aspects of non-verbal communication, including the use of ritual as a form of social communication, before going on to consider some of the more well-established mechanisms involved in the relatively superficial forms of person perception.

The chapter then looks at the way that people make sense out of the social worlds which they inhabit. On an individual level, it looks at the application of social schemas and scripts to social living, as well as the process of attribution. It then goes on to consider shared forms of social interpretation, including the process of social knowing referred to as lay epistemology, and the integrative approach to understanding shared beliefs and ideology provided by social representation theory.

Chapter summary

1. Non-verbal communication uses a range of cues, including facial expression, eye-contact, posture and gesture, proxemics, paralanguage and dress. These non-verbal cues can serve a number of different functions.

2. Ritual forms an important part of non-verbal communication. All human cultures involve some forms of ritual, and these can range from rigidly-prescribed large-scale social rituals to small individual aspects of patterning in behaviour.

3. Person perception can involve applying implicit personalities theories about which traits are likely to be found together, as well as the application of stereotypes and labels, personal constructs, and primacy effects.

4. People make sense out of their social worlds in a number of different ways. The concepts of schema, attribution and attitude have all been used to examine different aspects of social cognition.

5. Schemata affect our interpretations of social life, and help us to simplify our social worlds. Psychologists have studied four types of schema: event schemata, role schemata, person schemata and self-schemata.

6. Attribution theory concerns how people assign causes to events or actions. The fundamental attribution error is the way that we judge other people's behaviour as caused by their dispositions, but we see our own as being caused by the situation we are in.

7. Lay epistemology is concerned with the explanations and beliefs that people use in everyday living. In adopting particular beliefs, people are motivated by their need for structure, validity and specific conclusions.

8. Social representations are shared beliefs which are held by society in general or groups in society. They can often change over time, and can determine how information is accepted or applied in a social context.

LEARNING OBJECTIVES

1. **Non-verbal cues**
   The student shall be able to:
   - define terminology relating to non-verbal communication
   - identify non-verbal cues
   - describe functions of non-verbal communication

2. **Rituals**
   The student shall be able to:
   - identify functions of ritual in social interaction
   - link the study of ritual with other types of social analysis
   - apply the concept of ritual to everyday living

3. **Person perception**
   The student shall be able to:
   - define terms relating to person perception
   - describe factors which can influence person perception
   - describe a study of person perception

4. **Scripts and schemas**
   The student shall be able to:
   - identify different types of social schema
   - describe a study of social schemas
   - apply the concept of social scripts to everyday life

5. **Attribution**
   The student shall be able to:
   - define terms relating to attribution theory
   - describe a study of attributional error or bias
   - outline the major attributional theories

6. **Lay epistemology**
   The student shall be able to:
   - define terms relating to lay epistemology
   - identify factors influencing hypothesising in lay epistemology
   - outline motivational aspects of lay epistemology

7. **Social representations**
   The student shall be able to:
   - describe a study of social representations
   - identify mechanisms involved in the formation and
     maintenance of social representations
   - apply levels of explanation to theories in social psychology

Non-verbal cues

1. Cues of distance involved in NVC are known as:
(a) distal
(b) postural echo
(c) proxemics
(d) deportment

2. A non-verbal recognition cue is the _____

3. _____ often have culturally accepted meanings.

Rituals

4. Rituals often carry messages about _____ structures in society

5. Some conversations are examples of social _____ rather than ways of conveying information.

6. Eye-contact with the teacher on being asked a question in class usually signals that:
(a) the person doesn't understand the question
(b) the person doesn't know the answer
(c) the person is waiting for the class to end
(d) the person knows the answer

Person perception

7. Traits which can determine social judgements are known as _____ traits

8. The self-fulfilling _____
illustrates the dangers of having
expectations about a situation

9. In Luchins' study, people saw "Jim" as:
(a) morose and introverted
(b) sociable and extraverted
(c) whichever description came first
(d) whichever description came last

Scripts and schemas

10. Getting to know somebody involves
developing a _____ schema about
them

11. Zadny and Gerard found that after
watching a video people remembered:
(a) information about a burglary
(b) information about drug-taking
(c) information about people waiting for a
friend
(d) information which was relevant to
their schemas

12. The helpful behaviour shown in soap
operas can be seen as examples of social
_____ for everyday life

Attribution

13. A dispositional attribution is when we
conclude that an event is caused by:
(a) someone's individual personality
(b) interactions between the person and
the situation
(c) something in the situation
(d) a freak occurrence

14. Storms showed that people made more _____ attributions if they saw their own behaviour from another viewpoint

15. Kelly's three aspects of covariance are consistency, consensus and _____

Lay epistemology

16. Epistemology is the study of:
(a) knowledge
(b) beliefs
(c) understanding
(d) rugby players

17. Our hypothesis-generating capacity depends on recency and _____

18. Kruglanski argued that motivation depends on our need for structure, what we wish to believe, and our need for _____

Social representations

19. Di Giacomo showed that Belgian student activists failed to energise their colleagues because of differences in social _____

20. Moscovici suggested that social representations centre around a _____ nucleus

21. Social representations explain social behaviour on a cultural level, while non-verbal communication uses a _____ level

REVISION QUESTIONS

1. *Briefly describe the main non-verbal cues used in communication*

2. *Describe some of the basic mechanisms of person perception*

3. *Outline the correspondent inference approach to attribution theory*

ESSAY QUESTIONS

1. *Give evidence for or against the idea that non-verbal communication is more important than language for human beings*

2. *What psychological mechanisms do we use to make sense of the social world?*

3. *How important is an awareness of social representations for understanding human social action?*

USEFUL FURTHER READING

Hewstone, M., Stroebe, W., Codol, J-P & Stephenson, G. (1988) *Introduction to social psychology* Oxford: Blackwell

Argyle, M. (1988) *Bodily communication* (2nd ed.) London: Methuen

Hewstone, M. (1989) *Causal attribution: from cognitive processes to collective beliefs* Oxford: Blackwell

CHAPTER 15   SOCIAL INFLUENCE AND SOCIAL ACTION

The key issues
This chapter is concerned with social behaviour - how people act with one another, as opposed to social relationships or social understanding. It begins by looking at research into coaction and audience effects, before going on to consider the importance of social roles in social interaction. It then looks at aspects of social co-operation, including theories of leadership and conformity.

The chapter then continues its exploration of social behaviour by examining research into obedience and rebellion, before going on to look at helping behaviour and at some of the psychological factors which may act on or influence whether people are likely to help or co-operate with others, or not. It concludes by looking at behaviour in crowds, contrasting some very different theories of crowd behaviour.

Chapter summary

1. Research into coaction and audience effects shows that the presence of others affects what we do considerably. Social loafing can occur when efforts are shared with no individual recognition. Arousal, drives and distraction have been suggested as explanations for audience effects.

2. Social roles are important influences in both individual and group behaviour. One explanation for group polarisation is that group members adopt the position which they feel will present them most favourably to others.

3. Studies of leadership have focussed on different types of leader, leadership styles and the idea that effective leadership is about managing the expectations and values of the team.

4. Studies of conformity show that people tend to conform to group pressure rather than assert individual judgements. Kelman distinguished between compliance, internalisation and identification as mechanisms in conformity. Moscovici showed that minorities could have considerable influence on majority groups, if they maintained a consistent position.

5. Milgram's studies of obedience showed that many people will act cruelly if ordered to do so. Milgram proposed that people in hierarchies adopt an "agentic mode" in which their personal conscience is suppressed. However, past experience may also lead people to rebel against authority in accordance with their conscience.

6. People also often act to help others. Bystander intervention or otherwise is strongly influenced by people's definition of the situation, pluralistic ignorance, and diffusion of responsibility.

7. Latané's Law of Social Impact stated that the amount of social pressure on a person could be assessed by weighing up the intensity of social pressure, the number of people involved, and their immediate salience for the individual.

8. Early theories of crowds were that they acted as a primitive mob. Deindividuation theory formed a modern counterpart of this idea, but more recent studies suggest that crowd behaviour is more rational and structured than it is often presented as being.

LEARNING OBJECTIVES

1. **Coaction and audience effects**
    The student shall be able to:
    - describe a study of coaction or audience effects
    - outline explanations for audience effects
    - identify coaction or audience effects from examples

2. **Groups and roles**
   The student shall be able to:
   - define terminology related to the study of roles and groups
   - describe a study of social role or group behaviour
   - outline explanations for group polarisation

3. **Leadership**
   The student shall be able to:
   - distinguish between different types of leadership style
   - describe a study of leadership
   - outline major theories of leadership

4. **Conformity**
   The student shall be able to:
   - describe a study of conformity
   - identify factors contributing to conformity
   - outline types of conformity

5. **Obedience and rebellion**
   The student shall be able to:
   - describe a study of obedience or rebellion
   - identify factors likely to increase or reduce obedience
   - outline Milgram's theory of obedience

6. **Bystander intervention**
   The student shall be able to:
   - define terminology relating to bystander intervention
   - describe a study of helping behaviour
   - outline explanations for bystander behaviour

7. **Social impact**
   The student shall be able to:
   - outline Latané's theory of social impact
   - identify factors which will influence social impact
   - apply the theory of social impact to everyday life

8. **Crowds**
   The student shall be able to:
   - distinguish between theoretical models of aggression
   - describe a study of crowd behaviour or deindividuation
   - evaluate the deindividuation approach to crowd behaviour

OBJECTIVE QUESTIONS

Coaction

1. Paulus and Murdock found that the presence of an expert in an audience _____ audience effects

2. Baron suggested that audience effects occur because the person is:
(a) aided by interruption
(b) distracted from the task
(c) helped by encouragement
(d) unsure what to do

3. Performing music better on stage than when practising is an example of an _____ effect

Groups and roles

4. Punishment is a form of social _____

5. Stoner found that groups made _____ decisions than individuals

6. Festinger explained group polarisation in terms of:
(a) social identity
(b) social comparison
(c) social impact
(d) cognitive dissonance

Leadership

7. Laissez-faire leaders:
(a) direct followers in everything
(b) discuss what followers are to do
(c) allow discussion but make final decisions
(d) leave followers to do as they wish

8. When Lewin, Lippitt and White rotated different leaders around the groups, they found:
(a) everyone worked harder than they had done before
(b) the groups responded to the new leader's style
(c) only the authoritarian group worked hard
(d) the leader's style made no difference

9. Path-goal theory assumes that people:
(a) do not want leaders
(b) achieve goals without leaders
(c) live up to expectations of leaders
(d) need to be told what to do

Conformity

10. Allen and Levine's 1971 study investigated whether conformity was influenced by:
(a) the credibility of a minority opinion
(b) the timing of disagreement
(c) whether the disagreeing person shared the views of the research participant
(d) the number of people disagreeing

11. Moscovici and Faucheux found that _____ was the most important factor in minority influence

12. Going along with others but not changing your own opinions is known as _____

Obedience

13. Hofling studied obedience among
_____ in hospitals

14. Which of the following is not a factor
in obedience:
(a) distance
(b) situation
(c) gender
(d) responsibility

15. Milgram argued that when people are
working in hierarchies, they adopt:
(a) an agentic state
(b) an autonomous state
(c) an independent state
(d) children

Bystander intervention

16. Helping people is an example of
_____ behaviour

17. Latané and Rodin investigated
whether people would:
(a) assist someone who cried out for help
(b) report smoke coming from a ventilator
(c) give money to people to make a phone
call
(d) pay more for books sold for a good
reason

18. Failing to act because others are
present and could do so just as easily is
known as _____

Social impact

19. Latané argued that social forces can vary in strength, number and _____

20. Both _____ and peer groups can be an important factor in social impact

21. Which of the following would be least likely to illustrate the Law of Social Impact:
(a) giving money to someone begging in the street
(b) helping someone to push-start their car
(c) deciding to buy a pop record
(d) planning the timetable for a journey

Crowds

22. Freud attributed aggression to a form of energy called _____

23. Marsh et al. studied crowd behaviour by interviewing _____

24. Deindividuation has been criticised because:
(a) it depends on numbers
(b) it depends on personality
(c) it can be influenced by the situation
(d) it depends on attitudes

REVISION QUESTIONS

1. *Briefly describe research into group polarisation*

2. *What are the main factors in minority influence?*

3. *Outline Milgram's **theory** of obedience*

ESSAY QUESTIONS

1. *What is the psychological evidence for the idea that our behaviour is determined by the presence of other people?*

2. *Under what circumstances will people obey authority, and under what circumstances will they rebel?*

3. *Outline and discuss psychological evidence for or against the idea of "mob psychology"*

USEFUL FURTHER READING

Turner, J. C. (1991) *Social influence*   Milton Keynes: Open University Press

Brown, R. (1988) *Group processes: dynamics within and between groups* Oxford: Blackwell

Gaskell, G. & Benewick, R. (1987) *The crowd in contemporary Britain* London: Sage

The key issues

This chapter is concerned with research into attitudes and prejudice. It begins by exploring the different features and dimensions of attitudes, before going on to examine the apparent discrepancy between attitudes and behaviour, and some of the processes involved in attitude change. It then looks at research into the process of persuasion, largely in the context of advertising.

The chapter then goes on to consider the different theories which have been proposed as explanations for the social phenomenon known as prejudice, and some of the empirical research which has been put forward to support the different ideas about how prejudice occurs and is maintained. It ends by considering ten different principles of ethnic prejudice which have been suggested by existing psychological research.

Chapter summary

1. Attitudes are distinct from, but strongly linked to, personal values. An attitude may serve several different functions, including object appraisal, social adjustment, and the externalisation of inner conflicts.

2. Attitudes have three dimensions: a cognitive dimension, a conative (behavioural) dimension, and an affective dimension. There is often inconsistency between attitudes and behaviour. Fishbein and Ajzen argued that intentionality and expectations are important in directing behaviour, as well as attitudes.

3. Heider proposed that people like to keep their attitudes consistent and evenly balanced, and that this can be an important factor in interpersonal attitudes.

4. Assimilarity and contrast theory shows how we may be more receptive to attitudes similar to our own. Accentuation theory is concerned with how the social context affects how people present their attitudes. Labelling an attitude may mean that the person holds it more extremely than they did before.

5. Factors in persuasion include the source of the communication, the message itself, the person who is receiving the message, and the context in which the message is presented. Cognitive dissonance can also be a major factor in attitude change.

6. Theories of prejudice include biological explanation of prejudice, psychoanalytic explanations, and cultural explanations. The scapegoat theory of prejudice sees it as arising from the need to blame others for difficult economic circumstances.

7. Tajfel's early research on prejudice showed how categorisation, assimilation of social knowledge, and the search for coherent explanations can work together in producing social prejudice. Social identity theory emphasises how prejudice can develop out of perceived conflict between social groups.

8. Bethlehem's ten principles of ethnic prejudice show how cognitive mechanisms, social learning, intergroup and cultural factors all contribute to the manifestation of prejudice in society.

LEARNING OBJECTIVES

1. **Attitudes and values**
   The student shall be able to:
   - identify distinctive features of attitudes
   - distinguish between attitudes and values
   - list the major functions of attitudes

2. **Dimensions of attitudes**
   The student shall be able to:
   - distinguish between the three dimensions of attitudes
   - outline the theory of reasoned action
   - evaluate studies of attitudes and behaviour

3. **Cognitive balance**
   The student shall be able to:
   - define terms relating to cognitive balance theories
   - describe mechanisms of cognitive balance
   - apply principles of cognitive balance to everyday examples

4. **Social judgement theories**
   The student shall be able to:
   - define terms relating to social judgement theories
   - identify examples of social judgement mechanisms
   - describe a study of social judgement in attitudes

5. **Persuasion**
   The student shall be able to:
   - identify factors which can influence persuasion
   - outline the process of cognitive dissonance
   - describe a study of persuasion

6. **Prejudice**
   The student shall be able to:
   - identify major theories of prejudice
   - describe a study of prejudice
   - evaluate different explanations of prejudice

7. **Socio-cognitive theories of prejudice**
   The student shall be able to:
   - define terms relating to socio-cognitive theories of prejudice
   - describe social and cognitive processes underlying prejudice
   - list the stages of social discrimination

8. **Principles of ethnic prejudice**
   The student shall be able to:
   - list the principles of ethnic prejudice
   - describe a study illustrating principles of prejudice
   - evaluate studies of ethnic prejudice

Attitudes

1. Allport defined an attitude as "a mental and neural state of _____ "

2. Rokeach argued that values are more enduring than _____

3. Matching unconscious motives with what is going on around us is known as:
(a) object appraisal
(b) social adjustment
(c) social identification
(d) externalisation

Dimensions

4. Tone of voice and facial expressions both signal the _____ dimension of an attitude

5. The theory of reasoned action states that attitudes are less useful in predicting behaviour than:
(a) values
(b) possibilities
(c) beliefs
(d) intentions

6. Studies of attitudes and behaviour have been criticised because they:
(a) investigate specific actions not general ones
(b) investigate general actions not specific ones
(c) only investigate racist beliefs
(d) only produce specific conclusions

7. An example of dyadic balance would be:
(a) reciprocal liking between two people
(b) reciprocal liking between three people
(c) non-reciprocal liking between two people
(d) non-reciprocal liking between three people

8. People look for consistency between cognitions because an imbalance produces _____

9. John smokes, but knows that his classmates dislike smoking. In order to protect his self-esteem and preserve cognitive balance, he is likely to:
(a) agree that smoking is an unpleasant habit
(b) discount other people's opinions
(c) be dissatisfied with his habit
(d) only associate with non-smokers

10. The _____ effect is when we use our own positive views as a standard for positively evaluating other ideas

11. Labelling civil rights campaigners as "pinko liberals" is an example of:
(a) social conformity
(b) social facilitation
(c) social judgement
(d) social impact

12. Eiser compared _____ about information from different types of sources

Persuasion

13. The person who delivers a message is known as the _____ of the communication

14. Cognitive dissonance predicts that people will change their _____ if these are not congruent with their actions

15. Janis and Feshbach investigated persuasive messages about:
(a) personal hygiene
(b) dental hygiene
(c) modes of dress
(d) smoking

Prejudice

16. _____ theories see prejudices as arising from deep-set unconscious motives

17. Bagley and Verma compared racial prejudice in _____ and Britain

18. One problem with the authoritarian personality explanation of prejudice is that it concentrates on:
(a) individuals
(b) racism
(c) fascism
(d) recidivism

Social cognition

19. Exaggerating differences between one group and another is known as _____

20. The first stage in cognitive mechanisms of prejudice is _____

21. According to Allport, the first stage in social discrimination is:
(a) intergroup conflict
(b) accentuation
(c) categorisation
(d) anti-locution

Principles of prejudice

22. The third principle of ethnic prejudice is:
(a) stereotyping is more likely with less information
(b) education shows a negative relationship with prejudice
(c) children acquire prejudice from parents
(d) Prejudices change when social norms change

23. Sherif conducted a study of intergroup prejudice between boys at a _____

24. Sherif's study has been criticised because the intergroup _____ was contrived by the experimenters

REVISION QUESTIONS

1. *Describe the major functions of an attitude*

2. *Explain the concept of cognitive dissonance, and describe a study which illustrates it*

3. *Outline the cognitive dimensions of prejudice, as described by Tajfel*

ESSAY QUESTIONS

1. *How far can the concept of attitude dimensions further our understanding of persuasion?*

2. *Outline and evaluate theories of prejudice*

3. *How can prejudice between different social groups be reduced?*

USEFUL FURTHER READING

Hogg, M. A. & Abrams, D. (1988) *Social identifications: a social psychology of intergroup relations and group processes* London: Routledge

Hayes, N. (1993) *Principles of social psychology* Hove: Lawrence Erlbaum Associates

Bethlehem, D. W. (1985) *A social psychology of prejudice* London: Croom Helm

The key issues

This chapter is concerned with the way that cognition and skill develop from infancy onwards. It begins by looking at research into infant cognition and at some of the theories which have been put forward to explain the underlying mechanisms of infant cognitive development. It then goes on to consider theories of cognitive development during childhood, including some of the major reappraisals of Piaget's theory, and concluding with the idea that cognitive development might be understood in terms of the development of metacognitive skills.

The second half of the chapter is concerned with the general processes of skill acquisition. It begins by concerning itself primarily with physical skill acquisition, and the fundamental mechanisms which are involved in this process. From there, it goes on to consider theories of cognitive development as the acquisition of cognitive skills.

Chapter summary

1. Infants are born with a number of reflexes, which may be precursors to future behaviour, or simply left over from foetal activity in the womb. Some developmental psychologists see infant reflexes as providing the basis for future psychological development.

2. Research into infant perception includes studies of pattern and depth perception, and of reaching for object and defending against impact. They suggest that some level of perceptual organisation may be present at birth, but need further stimulation to develop.

3. Theories of infant cognition include the idea of cognition as resulting from operations on the environment, as distributed attention, as the fine-tuning of pre-adapted mechanisms, and as skill acquisition.

4. Piaget's theory of cognitive development emphasised the formation of schemata, through the results of operations on the environment. Different types of operations became possible as a result of the gradual reduction of egocentricity.

5. Empirical reappraisals of Piaget's work uncovered a number of methodological weaknesses, which may have resulted in a serious under-estimation of children's cognitive abilities. Children develop metacognitive skills from quite an early age, and these become more sophisticated through childhood.

6. Early models of skill acquisition saw it as stimulus-response links or information processing. Recent ones see complex skills as hierarchies of motor schemas. Research into skill acquisition has emphasised the effects of types of practice, the need for knowledge of results, explorations of the speed / accuracy tradeoff, and the process of automatisation.

7. Bruner and Fischer both proposed that cognitive development proceeds through the acquisition of skills. Bruner emphasised the role of intentionality, automatisation and modularisation in cognitive skill development.

8. Fischer's hierarchical model of cognitive skill development described how sensori-motor skills led to representational skills, which in turn led to the development of abstract skills.

LEARNING OBJECTIVES

1. **Infant reflexes**
   The student shall be able to:
   - identify common infant reflexes
   - distinguish between theories of infant reflexes
   - link infant reflexes with later development

2. **Infant perception**
   The student shall be able to:
   - identify different aspects of infant perception
   - describe a study of infant perception
   - evaluate research into infant perception

3. **Theories of infant cognition**
   The student shall be able to:
   - define terms relating to theories of infant cognition
   - outline the four major theories of infant cognition
   - apply theories of infant cognition to instances of infant behaviour

4. **Piaget**
   The student shall be able to:
   - define terms relating to Piagetian theory
   - describe Piaget's basic studies of cognition
   - explain basic Piagetian processes

5. **Reappraisals of Piaget**
   The student shall be able to:
   - describe a study reappraising Piagetian ideas
   - evaluate the Piagetian approach to cognitive development
   - outline alternatives to Piagetian theory

6. **Skill acquisition**
   The student shall be able to:
   - list the features of skilled behaviour
   - describe theories of skill acquisition
   - identify factors which can influence skill acquisition

7. **Models of skill acquisition**
   The student shall be able to:
   - define terms relating to theories of skill acquisition
   - outline the processes of skill acquisition
   - contrast different models of skill acquisition

OBJECTIVE QUESTIONS

Infant reflexes

1. The _____ reflex occurs when an infant's head drops suddenly

2. Infant reflexes have been seen as either precursors to future activity, or as _____ from pre-birth activity

3. It is possible that the stepping reflex:
(a) prevents the infant from walking
(b) helps to establish right-left leg co-ordination
(c) does not actually happen
(d) is retained for six months

Infant perception

4. The ability to distinguish figures against backgrounds is part of _____ perception

5. Bower used _____ as the reward in studies of infant size constancy

6. One problem with Gibson and Walk's use of the visual cliff to study infant depth perception was:
(a) that the infants were too old
(b) that the infants were too young
(c) that the infants were too small
(d) that the infants were too large

7. An organised act by an infant which produces stimulation which re-elicits the act is known as a _____

8. J. J. Gibson believed that infant cognition was all about:
(a) skill acquisition
(b) distributed attention
(c) operating on the environment
(d) fine-tuning pre-adapted mechanisms

9. An infant becoming better at recognising its mother can be seen as _____ pre-adapted perceptual mechanisms

10. Genetic epistemology is about:
(a) the evolutionary origins of knowledge
(b) knowledge about genes and chromosomes
(c) Eysenck's theory of personality
(d) the nature-nurture debate

11. Piaget showed that children who were unable to _____ could not pick out a photograph showing a doll's view of some model mountains

12. Schemata are formed through _____ and accommodation

13. Bower and Wishart showed that:
(a) infants would not reach for objects in the dark
(b) children could get the right answer if they were only asked once
(c) infants would still reach for objects in the dark
(d) if "naughty teddy" changed things, children got the answer right

14. Piagetian theory has been criticised because:
(a) it only deals with children and not adults
(b) it under-estimates children's social knowledge
(c) it doesn't apply to moral development
(d) it involves schemas

15. Being able to monitor our own perceptual and memory processes is an aspect of _____

Skill acquisition

16. Which of the following is not a feature of skilled behaviour:
(a) goal-directed
(b) achieved with economy of time and effort
(c) requires concentration
(d) acquired by practice

17. Annett described skill acquisition as the _____ organisation of motor programs

18. Which of the following does not influence skill acquisition:
(a) feedback
(b) practice
(c) whole or part learning
(d) computer simulation

Theories of skill acquisition

19. In Fischer's theory, the orienting of attention towards different stimuli is known as _____

20. Bruner saw the _____ of behaviour into skilled units as the core of skill development

21. Fischer saw hierarchical skill systems as the basis for cognitive development, whereas Piaget used the concept of

_____

REVISION QUESTIONS

1. *Can infants perceive depth?*

2. *Describe the basic processes involved in the formation of schemata*

3. *Outline Fischer's theory of skill development*

ESSAY QUESTIONS

1. *What can experimental evidence tell us about infant cognition?*

2. *Critically evaluate Piaget's theory of cognitive development*

3. *What are the main processes involved in human skill acquisition?*

USEFUL FURTHER READING

Bremner, G. (1988) *Infancy* Oxford: Blackwell

Donaldson, M. (1978) *Children's minds* London: Fontana

Schmidt, R. (1991) *Motor learning and performance: from principle to practice* Champagne, Ill.: Human Kinetics Books

CHAPTER 18   PERSONAL DEVELOPMENT

The key issues

This chapter is concerned with the way that personal development is firmly located in a social network. It begins by exploring aspects of infant sociability, and the way that the quality of parent-infant interaction determines the nature of the attachment which an infant develops with its caretakers. From there, it considers ideas about the importance of stable and secure relationships, and questions of recovery from early deprivation.

The chapter then goes on to consider the way that the child develops social responsibility, and an awareness of other people. It looks at the importance of interactions within the child's family, and at the way that the young child develops a theory of mind which enables it to understand how others may be thinking or feeling. Autistic children appear to miss out on this development. The chapter concludes by looking at children's ideas about friendship, and at stage theories of moral development through later childhood.

Chapter summary

1. Early theories of attachment were based on the idea of imprinting: that the infant forms a rapid, exclusive bond with its mother shortly after birth, and that other relationships are less important.

2. Later research into human attachments showed that they develop as a result of parent-infant interaction. The human infant is innately predisposed to respond positively to interactions with other human beings.

3. Depending on the quality of interaction which they have with their parents, human infants may show secure, insecure or ambivalent attachments. These involve different behaviour and transactions between the parent and infant.

4. The continuity hypothesis states that early experience exerts a permanent effect on adult personality. However, research implies that it is possible to recover from even very severely deprived childhoods, as long as the person experiences help and warm relationships in later life.

5. Teasing, comforting and responding to distress are important aspects of forming relationships with other people. Children develop a theory of mind - an awareness that other people have minds of their own - which is an important feature of social interaction and relationships.

6. Autistic children may not develop a theory of mind. Research shows that they find it difficult to interpret social situations which require such knowledge, and that they interact very directly with their world without taking into account what other people may know or believe.

7. Stage theories of moral development were put forward by both Piaget and Kohlberg. More recent research, however, has emphasised the socio-cognitive aspects of moral development rather than documenting stages.

LEARNING OBJECTIVES

1. **Imprinting and monotropy**
The student shall be able to:
- identify key concepts in early models of attachment
- describe a study of maternal deprivation
- evaluate evidence for maternal deprivation

2. **Parent-infant interaction**
The student shall be able to:
- identify distinctive features of infant sociability
- describe a study of infant sociability
- outline aspects of parenting behaviour

3. **Secure and insecure attachment**
The student shall be able to:
- list the short-term response to separation
- identify aspects of infant behaviour in cases of insecurity
- describe underlying mechanisms in infant relationships

4. **Recovery in later life**
The student shall be able to:
- describe a study of recovery from disturbed childhood
- identify important features of recovery from disturbed childhood
- evaluate evidence for recovery from severe deprivation

5. **Developing social awareness**
The student shall be able to:
- identify features of social interaction in the home
- describe a study of the child's theory of mind
- outline age-related changes in social awareness

6. **Autism**
The student shall be able to:
- list features of childhood autism
- distinguish between behaviours shown by normal and autistic children
- link an absence of theory of mind with autistic behaviour

7. **Moral development**
The student shall be able to:
- outline how children perceive friendship
- list stages of moral development
- describe a study of socio-cognitive development

OBJECTIVE QUESTIONS

Imprinting

1. Monotropy is:
(a) the process of attachment shown by young ducks
(b) the relationships between siblings in a family
(c) the idea that an infant develops a special, qualitatively different relationship with its mother
(d) the ability of infants to form relationships with more than one person

2. Goldfarb found that children who grew up in institutions were less rule-abiding, less sociable, and less _____

3. Rutter showed that juvenile delinquency was most likely to be associated with _____ in the family home

Parent-infant interaction

4. Patterns of interaction between parent and infant often take the form of whole sequences of behaviour known as

_____

5. Stern found that parents and infants _____ each other's facial expressions

6. Yogman found that:
(a) fathers only interacted with their infants when they were alone
(b) fathers interacted in short bursts with their infants
(c) fathers interacted continuously with their infants
(d) fathers did not interact with their infants

Insecure attachment

7. The second-stage response to short-term separation is _____

8. Infants in avoidant relationships maintain _____ levels of contact

9. Which of the following was not one the behavioural systems identified by Bowlby:
(a) the affiliation system
(b) the social system
(c) the fear / wariness system
(d) the attachment system

Recovery

10. Roe found no difference in adulthood between a control group and 36 people who had suffered from parental _____ , abuse, or chronic alcoholism in childhood

11. People can recover from disturbed childhoods as long as they have:
(a) emotionally secure relationships in later life
(b) freedom from stress in later life
(c) financially secure relationships in later life
(d) children in later life

12. Rutter argued that studies which supported the _____ hypothesis did not look at whether the stressful experiences had continued in later childhood or not

Social awareness

13. Dunn claimed that learning to cope with teasing:
(a) handicaps children in later life
(b) helps children to develop social competence
(c) causes permanent distress in children
(d) produces insecure attachments

14. Perner studied children's awareness of false beliefs by hiding a pencil in a _____

15. Comforting others by offering them an object appears at approximately:
(a) 10 - 12 months
(b) 12 - 18 months
(c) 18 - 24 months
(d) 24 - 36 months

Autism

16. Which of the following is a symptom of childhood autism:
(a) lack of size constancy
(b) delayed walking
(c) lack of spontaneous play
(d) lack of bladder control

17. Hobson showed that autistic children were unable to interpret _____ in facial expressions

18. _____ children are unable to predict what someone else will be thinking

Moral development

19. Which of the following was identified by 6-8 years olds as a way of increasing liking:
(a) increased time spent together
(b) playing games together
(c) increased sharing of possessions
(d) only having one friend

20. Kohlberg's third stage of moral development is that of _____ morality

21. Siegel and Storey found that experienced nursery school children could distinguish between _____ and moral transgressions, whereas novices couldn't

REVISION QUESTIONS

1. *Outline significant aspects of parent-infant interaction*

2. *Briefly describe Ainsworth's research into secure and insecure attachment*

3. *Describe the characteristics of autistic behaviour*

ESSAY QUESTIONS

1. *Using psychological evidence, discuss whether early experience inevitably affects the rest of one's life*

2. *What have psychologists discovered about the child's theory of mind?*

3. *Compare stage theories of moral development with socio-cognitive approaches*

USEFUL FURTHER READING

Rutter, M. & Rutter, M. (1992) *Developing minds: challenge and continuity across the life span* Harmondsworth: Penguin

Dunn, J. (1988) *The beginnings of social understanding* Oxford: Blackwell

Harris, P. L. (1989) *Children and emotion: the development of psychological understanding* Oxford: Blackwell

The key issues

This chapter is concerned with how the child acquires the forms of social awareness and understanding which it will need to interact with wider society. It begins by looking at the many different mechanisms by which the child develops, including fundamental learning and maturational processes as well as social mechanisms. It then goes on to consider achievement motivation and play, since both of these can be considered to be important mechanisms of child development.

The chapter continues by exploring the child's acquisition of gender role, and the various theories which have been put forward to suggest how this happens. The final part of the chapter is concerned with the acquisition of language, since this represents the primary medium of cultural and social transmission. Different theories of language acquisition are explored, as is the relationship between language and thinking, and the development of metalinguistic awareness.

Chapter summary

1. The basic mechanisms by which children develop psychologically include genetic maturation, conditioning, imitation and identification, metacognition and social cognition, the formation of self-efficacy beliefs and responses to social expectations.

2. The study of achievement motivation has moved from early attempts to identify internal personality traits, to approaches which emphasised child-rearing styles, and on to the way that the child's own attributions and goals can affect their efforts.

3. A number of researchers have attempted to identify stages in children's play, or categories of different types of play. Other researchers have identified distinctive features of play, such as intrinsic motivation, its process rather than product-centred nature; its concern with non-literal behaviours, and its self-directed nature.

4. Classic theories of play include play as surplus energy, play as relaxation, play as recapitulation, and play as practice. More recent approaches see play as the expression of underlying psychodynamic conflict, as stimulus-seeking, as metacommunication, as social framing, and as meta-representation.

5. Psychological research into how the child comes to acquire appropriate gender role behaviour includes biological, bio-social, social learning, and psychoanalytic approaches, and research which emphasises gender similarity and androgeny.

6. Theories of language acquisition include the nature-nurture debate between Chomsky and Skinner, and the more recent approach which emphasises the role of human social contact in language learning.

7. There have been several different approaches to the relationship between language and thinking. Piaget saw language as entirely dependent on thought, simply reflecting the child's thinking; Bruner saw language as a tool which amplifies and augments thought.

8. Vygotsky saw language and thought as having separate functions: language as a social skill, concerned with social interaction, and thought as the child's way of making sense out of the world.

9. Metalinguistic research shows that the child develops a sophisticated awareness of the appropriate use of language from quite an early age. The use of rhymes and word-games may heighten metalinguistic awareness, and facilitate reading development.

LEARNING OBJECTIVES
1. **Mechanisms of development**
    The student shall be able to:
    - define terms relating to mechanisms of development
    - describe individual mechanisms of development
    - outline social mechanisms of development

2.   **Achievement motivation**
      The student shall be able to:
      - identify factors in achievement motivation
      - describe a study of achievement motivation
      - distinguish between trait and social theories

3.   **Classifications of play**
      The student shall be able to:
      - list different types of play
      - describe distinctive features of play
      - evaluate definitions of play

4.   **Theories of play**
      The student shall be able to:
      - define terms relating to theories of play
      - describe different theories of play
      - evaluate theories of play

5.   **Gender role**
      The student shall be able to:
      - define terms relating to the study of gender role
      - describe a study of gender role acquisition
      - distinguish types of explanation for gender role

6.   **Language acquisition**
      The student shall be able to:
      - identify potential mechanisms of language acquisition
      - describe major theories of language acquisition
      - evaluate theories of language acquisition

7.   **Language and thinking**
      The student shall be able to:
      - identify functions of language and thinking
      - distinguish between Piaget's and Bruner's explanations
      - apply models of language and thinking to everyday life

8.   **Vygotsky's theory of language**
      The student shall be able to:
      - describe processes of language and thinking in Vygotsky's model
      - identify functions of language and thinking in Vygotsky's model
      - apply Vygotsky's model to everyday experience

9. Metalinguistics

The student shall be able to:
- define terms relating to metalinguistic awareness
- identify factors which can enhance metalinguistic skills
- describe a study of metalinguistic awareness

OBJECTIVE QUESTIONS

Mechanisms

1. Learning as a result of seeing other people being rewarded is known as _____ learning

2. Genetic maturation is:
(a) when a child reaches puberty
(b) genetic factors in knowledge
(c) the same genetic engineering
(d) development which is determined by the genes

3. Something which happens because people have predicted that it will occur is known as a _____

Achievement motivation

4. _____ about how success happens are an important factor in achievement motivation

5. Rosen and d'Andrade asked blindfolded children to:
(a) walk a tightrope
(b) build a tower
(c) complete a story
(d) run a race

6. Social explanations for achievement motivation often focus on parental _____

Classifications of play

7. Parton classified turn-taking in play as an example of:
(a) parallel play
(b) associative play
(c) co-operative play
(d) onlooker play

8. Garvey defined play as activity which is free from _____ imposed rules

9. Cohen argued that studying play in _____ was more valid than studying play in nursery schools

Theories of play

10. Neoteny is the idea that we are born:
(a) to older parents
(b) too small
(c) with perceptual abilities
(d) at a premature stage of development

11. The idea that play provides a context or frame for interaction is the _____ theory of play

12. The _____ theory of play has been criticised because children sometimes play to exhaustion

Gender role

13. Having the psychological characteristics of both males and females is known as:
(a) androgyny
(b) transsexualism
(c) hermaphroditism
(d) heterosexuality

14. Smith and Lloyd showed that people treated babies:
(a) differently if they were dressed as girl or boy
(b) aggressively if they were dressed as little girls
(c) passively if they were dressed as little boys
(d) the same if they were dressed as girl or boy

15. Bem's explanation for gender role acquisition is:
(a) bio-social
(b) psychoanalytic
(c) social learning
(d) biological

Language acquisition

16. Chomsky's proposed mechanism for language acquisition was the:
(a) LDA
(b) LAS
(c) UCS
(d) LAD

17. Skinner believed that language could be understood simply as _____ behaviour

18. The idea of language as developing during a _____ was challenged by the discovery of Genie

Language and thinking

19. Piaget believed that language:
(a) reflected thought
(b) stimulated thought
(c) was different from thought
(d) was all that existed

20. Bruner did not agree with Piaget's idea that the reduction of _____ was the core of both language and cognitive development

21. _____ believed that we use words as symbols to represent our experience

Vygotsky

22. Vygotsky saw language as a social process, while thinking was a _____ one

23. Vygotsky believed that the bridge between thought and language was:
(a) inner speech
(b) outer speech
(c) egocentric speech
(d) latent speech

24. According to Vygotsky, a child talking aloud as it plays is using language as a _____ tool and not for communication

Metalinguistics

25. Semantic rules are rules about:
(a) language
(b) meaning
(c) grammar
(d) metaphors

26. _____ play can enhance metalinguistic skills

27. Winner et al. studied how children understand:
(a) nursery rhymes
(b) conversations
(c) poems
(d) metaphors

REVISION QUESTIONS

1.   *What factors influence achievement motivation in children?*

2.   *Outline the major theories of gender-role acquisition*

3.   *Briefly describe the Skinner-Chomsky debate on language acquisition*

ESSAY QUESTIONS

1.   *Outline the fundamental processes and mechanisms underlying the child's psychological development*

2.   *Critically evaluate psychological research into children's play*

3.   *Outline and evaluate Vygotsky's theory of child language*

USEFUL FURTHER READING

McGurk et al. (eds) (1992) *Childhood social development* Hove: Lawrence Erlbaum Associates

Cohen, D. (1992) *The development of play* (2nd ed.) London: Routledge

Lock, A. & Fisher, E. (1984) *Language development* Milton Keynes: Open University Press

The key issues

This chapter is concerned with how people develop through the lifespan. It begins by examining some of the assumptions of the lifespan approach, before going on to a more detailed consideration of the various theories of adolescence which have been put forward by psychologists. The idea of adolescence as a period of "storm and stress" is particularly challenged.

The chapter then goes on to consider life-transitions during adulthood, and the implications of stressful life-events to psychological well-being. It then looks at issues of dying and bereavement, and at what is involved in the process of grieving. Finally, it looks at the different approaches to understanding old age and retirement, and at how different theoretical perspectives have resulted in very different recommendations for this period of life.

Chapter summary

1. Lifespan psychology assumes that development needs to be viewed within its social context. It sees people as active agents in shaping their own lives, exerting a reciprocal influence on their physical and social environments.

2. One of the most influential views of adolescence has been that it is a period of storm and stress, producing disruption and emotional upheaval for the adolescent. But more recent research suggests that this applies only to a minority of adolescents.

3. Alternative perspectives on adolescence have emphasised the role transitions of adolescence, or seen it as a developmental stage in which a coherent identity must be built.

4. Coleman's focal theory of adolescence proposes that adolescence is a period which involves diverse changes in many, if not all, areas of life, and that the individual focusses on different changes at different times during the adolescent period.

5. Some studies of adulthood have looked at it in terms of stages, seasons, or in terms of changes in consciousness. The idea of the family life-cycle highlights different phases through which families pass, but has been criticised because it does not take account of single parenting, divorce, or remarriage.

6. Stressful life-events may have deleterious effects on the individual's physical health. However, these can be ameliorated by lifestyle or appropriate coping mechanisms.

7. Bereavement has three stages: numbness, pining, and depression. Abnormally prolonged grieving may result if the normal grieving process is interrupted or prevented. Research into dying suggests that openness is one of the most important psychological factors in coping with death.

8. Ageing is subject to many social stereotypes, few of which appear to be realistic. Research evidence suggests that both physical and mental skills and abilities can improve with age if they are practised: they do not automatically decline.

9. Explanations for why old people become less visible in society after retirement include disengagement theory, activity theory, and social exchange theory.

LEARNING OBJECTIVES

1. **The lifespan approach**
   The student shall be able to:
   - define terms relating to lifespan psychology
   - list the four assumptions of the lifespan approach
   - apply lifespan concepts to everyday experience

2.   **Adolescence as storm and stress**
The student shall be able to:
- outline mechanisms leading to emotional disruption during adolescence
- describe theories of adolescence as emotional upheaval
- evaluate the storm and stress model of adolescence

3.   **Alternative theories of adolescence**
The student shall be able to:
- define terms relating to alternative models of adolescence
- list Erikson's stages of development
- apply concepts of role transition to everyday examples

4.   **Stage theories of adulthood**
The student shall be able to:
- list stages of the family life-cycle
- describe theories of adulthood
- evaluate theories of adulthood and family life

5.   **Stressful life-events**
The student shall be able to:
- outline the stressful life-events model
- describe a study of stressful life-events and/or coping
- evaluate the stressful life-events approach

6.   **Grieving and bereavement**
The student shall be able to:
- list the stages and components of grief
- distinguish between normal and abnormal grieving
- describe social factors which can influence the experience of dying

7.   **Experience and ageing**
The student shall be able to:
- describe a study of ageing and ability
- identify factors which can mitigate the effects of ageing
- evaluate common assumptions about ageing

8.   **Theories of retirement**
The student shall be able to:
- list the phases of retirement
- describe theories of retirement
- evaluate theories of retirement

OBJECTIVE QUESTIONS

Lifespan approach

1. When two or more people influence one another, the influence is known as

_____

2. Lifespan psychology assumes that people are active _____ in their own lives

3. The psychology of ageing needs to be seen in a _____ context as well as a physical one

Storm and stress

4. Blos attributed adolescent emotional disruption to the process of _____

5. The concept of a youth culture arises from which approach to adolescence:
(a) psychoanalytic
(b) biological
(c) maturational
(d) cultural relativity

6. Bandura challenged the storm and stress model of adolescence on the grounds that:
(a) there was too much of it in the media
(b) most adolescents didn't experience it
(c) it was too widespread to be of any use
(d) it was psychoanalytic in origin

Other theories

7. A period in which life-decisions are left in abeyance is known as a _____

8. Erikson's third developmental conflict is _____

9. A student leaving home and going to university is an example of:
(a) role conflict
(b) role confusion
(c) identity diffusion
(d) role transition

Adulthood

10. The third stage in the family life-cycle is:
(a) nurturing period
(b) empty-nest period
(c) authority period
(d) honeymoon period

11. Levinson identified eight _____ of adulthood

12. Duvall's model gave structure to the way that we research the _____ .

Stressful life-events

13. A high level of stressful life-events is a predictor of future _____ problems

14. Strack et al. (1985) asked people to think about:
(a) past events
(b) future events
(c) shopping lists
(d) the family life-cycle

15. The stressful life-events scale has been criticised because:
(a) some of the correlations were very small
(b) it doesn't take account of single parent families
(c) it is really all about role conflicts
(d) it deals with differences not correlations

Bereavement

16. Refusing to acknowledge that someone has died is known as _____

17. Normal and abnormal grieving can be distinguished by:
(a) the amount of crying
(b) the person's relationship with the deceased
(c) insomnia
(d) length of time spent in intense grief

18. One of the main problems associated with dying is people's reluctance to _____ about it

Ageing

19. Burns studied how teachers' _____ changed as they grew older

20. Which of these describes the effect of practice on ageing:
(a) it reduces it
(b) it mitigates it
(c) it increases it
(d) it has no effect on it

21. Welford found that lower performance among older people was not lack of ability, but lack of _____

Retirement

22. Atchley's fourth phase of retirement is:
(a) disenchantment phase
(b) disengagement phase
(c) reorientation phase
(d) adjusted phase

23. The idea that people should remain involved in society when they retire is known as _____ theory

24. Disengagement theory has been criticised because:
(a) it doesn't account for all old people
(b) it is a psychosocial theory
(c) it stresses new roles and activities
(d) it only applies to married people

REVISION QUESTIONS

1. *Describe Coleman's focal theory of adolescence*

2. *Briefly describe research into stressful life-events*

3. *Outline the stages of response to bereavement*

ESSAY QUESTIONS

1. *Is adolescence inevitably a period of "storm and stress"? Give psychological evidence for your answer*

2. *Compare and contrast stage, season and family life-cycle models of adult development*

3. *"Ageing is nothing but disengagement and decline". Do you agree? Give psychological evidence for your answer*

USEFUL FURTHER READING

Coleman, J. C. & Hendry, L. (1980) *The nature of adolescence* (2nd ed.) London: Routledge

Sugarman, L. (1986) *Life-span development: concepts, theories and interventions* London: Methuen

Owens, G. & Naylor, F. (1989) *Living while dying* Wellingborough: Thorsons

CHAPTER 21   INTRODUCING COMPARATIVE PSYCHOLOGY

The key issues

This chapter is concerned with the fundamental mechanisms which underpin animal behaviour. It begins with an introduction to comparative psychology and some of its fundamental concepts, and goes on to look at the theory of evolution, and some of its associated concepts such as biodiversity and phylogeny.

The chapter then looks at the mechanisms involved in animal behaviour. It begins with genetic transmission, and looks at the characteristics of inherited behaviour and how such behaviour is elicited. It then goes on to examine the principles involved in classical and operant conditioning, and some other forms of learning, before concluding by exploring the potential integration of genetic and learned influences on behaviour.

Chapter summary

1. Comparative psychology is concerned with animal behaviour. Fundamental concepts in comparative psychology include Lloyd Morgan's canon, which states that the lowest possible level of explanation should be used.

2. The theory of evolution is basic to comparative psychology. It includes the principles of biodiversity and behavioural diversity, genetic transmission, and, more cautiously, the idea of the phylogenetic scale.

3. Genetically controlled behaviour takes the form of fixed action patterns, which appear as a result of maturation. They are shown when a sign stimulus triggers an innate releasing mechanism.

4. The hydraulic model of instinctive behaviour suggests that there is a reservoir of action-specific energy which is released in the form of fixed action patterns. This idea was challenged by later researchers.

5. Classical conditioning occurs as a result of association of a stimulus with an involuntary response to a different stimulus. Recent research into classical conditioning suggests that expectation is also important in this form of learning.

6. Operant conditioning occurs when behaviour has a pleasant effect, either through reward, or by escaping or avoiding an aversive stimulus. Reinforcement is a central concept in operant conditioning. Recent research suggests that it too involves some cognitive processing.

7. Studies of one-trial learning show that some forms of learning are easier than others. This appears to be an indication of genetic preparedness to learn survival-oriented behaviour. Other forms of learning include insight learning, the formation of learning sets, latent learning and cognitive maps.

8. It is possible to see a number of intermediate stages in the control of behaviour between genetically determined behaviour and learned behaviour. These intermediate stages include forms of preparedness in learning, and critical and sensitive periods.

LEARNING OBJECTIVES

1. **Fundamental concepts**
    The student shall be able to:
    - identify significant issues in comparative psychology
    - describe fundamental concepts in comparative psychology
    - apply comparative concepts to examples of animal behaviour

2. **Evolution**
   The student shall be able to:
   - describe the basic processes of evolution
   - identify concepts in evolutionary theory
   - outline the principles of genetic transmission

3. **Genetically controlled behaviour**
   The student shall be able to:
   - list criteria for genetically controlled behaviour
   - describe mechanisms of genetically controlled behaviour
   - apply principles of genetic control of behaviour to specific examples

4. **Theories of inherited behaviour**
   The student shall be able to:
   - define terms relating to models of inherited behaviour
   - describe hydraulic models of inherited behaviour
   - evaluate hydraulic models of inherited behaviour

5. **Classical conditioning**
   The student shall be able to:
   - define terms relating to classical conditioning
   - describe the processes involved in classical conditioning
   - evaluate behaviourist explanations for classical conditioning

6. **Operant conditioning**
   The student shall be able to:
   - define terms relating to operant conditioning
   - describe features of operant conditioning
   - link principles of operant conditioning with specific examples

7. **Types of learning**
   The student shall be able to:
   - outline different types of learning
   - describe a study of animal learning
   - apply concepts of learning to everyday examples

8. **Genetically prepared learning**
   The student shall be able to:
   - identify examples of genetically prepared learning
   - describe a study of genetically prepared learning
   - identify adaptive principles in genetically prepared learning

OBJECTIVE QUESTIONS

Fundamental concepts

1. Tinbergen identified development, functions, _____ and evolution as the four areas of comparative psychology

2. Attributing human emotions and intentions to animals is called:
(a) extrapolation
(b) deindividuation
(c) anthropomorphism
(d) recidivism

3. Describing a dog's behaviour as "dominant" is an example of describing behaviour:
(a) in terms of its environmental effects
(b) in terms of patterns of movement
(c) animistically
(d) using Lloyd Morgan's Canon

Evolution

4. Darwin believed that evolution occurred through:
(a) genetic engineering
(b) genetic transmission
(c) learning processes
(d) natural selection

5. The evolutionary history of a species is known as its _____

6. The common abbreviation for the main type of genetic material is _____

Genetics

7. Lorenz and Tinbergen's fourth criterion for genetically controlled behaviour is that it should not need to be _____

8. Fixed action patterns are released by:
(a) phylogeny
(b) genetic transmission
(c) learned releasing mechanisms
(d) innate releasing mechanisms

9. Aggressive behaviour in the stickleback is triggered by _____ objects

Inherited behaviour

10. Stopping an aggressive display and performing an irrelevant action is known as _____

11. In Lorenz's model of inherited behaviour, the sign stimulus triggers the IRM, which releases _____ energy

12. Bastock et al. suggested that the idea of _____ is preferable to that of a consummatory act

Classical conditioning

13. _____ is when a response is given to a previously reinforced stimulus but not a non-reinforced one

14. Classical conditioning is based on associating:
(a) UCS and UCR
(b) UCS and CR
(c) UCS and CS
(d) CS and CR

15. Rescorla argued that the ability to _____ what will happen next is more important than temporal contiguity

Operant conditioning

16. A _____ reinforcer works by being associated with a primary reinforcer

17. Negative reinforcement is:
(a) avoiding unpleasant stimuli
(b) receiving an unpleasant response
(c) never having to say you're sorry
(d) learning to do something unpleasant

18. Token economy is based on the principle that reinforcement must happen _____ after the behaviour

Types of learning

19. Tolman showed that learning involved a _____ element

20. Köhler studied problem-solving in _____

21. Learning how to do IQ tests by practising could be an example of:
(a) latent learning
(b) operant conditioning
(c) insight learning
(d) learning sets

Prepared learning

22. _____ and sensitive periods are genetically prepared learning mechanisms

23. Curio et al. showed that blackbirds learn _____ by imitation

24. Disliking food which once made you sick is adaptive because:
(a) it may have been badly cooked
(b) such food might be poisonous
(c) being sick is bad for you
(d) it is negative reinforcement

REVISION QUESTIONS

1.   *Outline the distinctive features of instinctive behaviour*

2.   *Describe the main principles of operant conditioning*

3.   *Describe one example of genetically prepared learning*

ESSAY QUESTIONS

1.   *Giving examples, describe the basic mechanisms by which different species evolve*

2.   *From the comparative evidence, is it true to say that both reinforcement and punishment are necessary for learning?*

3.   *"All learning is genetic in origin". Using comparative evidence, explain and evaluate this statement.*

USEFUL FURTHER READING

Gould, S. J. (1978) *Ever since Darwin: reflections in natural history*
Harmondsworth: Penguin

Gonick, L. & Wheelis, M. (1991) *The cartoon guide to genetics* (2nd ed.)
New York: Harper Collins

Walker, S. (1984) *Learning theory and behaviour modification* London:
Methuen

The key issues

This chapter looks at some of the main topics which have been explored by comparative psychologists and ethologists. It begins by looking at perspectives on courtship and mating, and goes on to consider the mechanisms of imprinting and other forms of animal attachment, and some examples of parental behaviour in different species.

The chapter then goes on to consider different manifestations of social structure, including the question of territoriality, issues of dominance and social organisation, and research into aggression and reconciliation. It concludes by looking at some of the different versions of evolutionary theory which have been proposed in explanation for these observations.

Chapter summary

1. Explanations for courtship rituals include courtship as ensuring appropriate pairing, as permitting survival of individuals, as displays of individual fitness, as improving the species, and as strengthening pair-bonding. Examples of animal courtship fitting each of these explanations can be found.

2. Imprinting is a special form of learning in which a young precocial animal identifies a parent figure during a sensitive period, and subsequently follows it around. Research into imprinting has produced the law of effort, and some debate about the lasting nature of its effects.

3. Studies of attachment in rhesus monkeys showed that the most important factor for normal social development was contact with other members of the species.

4. Studies of parental behaviour in mammals show that it is generally a combination of inherited and learned components, and becomes more variable as we move higher up the phylogenetic scale.

5. Studies of social organisation in primates suggest that dominance behaviour may be intimately linked with environmental demands. Metaphors and assumptions can influence research in this area. Linear pecking orders may be much less common than were once supposed.

6. There are a number of different types of territoriality, including nested territories and territories within larger colonies. Most species seem to show seasonal territoriality. Territorial displays are linked with courtship, and may involve the ritualised display of natural weaponry.

7. Research into territoriality, includes the idea of territory as linked with natural resources, and game theory models of territorial behaviour. Another possibility is to see territoriality as a display of resource holding power on the part of the animal.

8. Lorenz construed animal aggression as a manifestation of an innate drive, channelled into a ritualised display. This may have led us to overlook the importance of reconciliation in social behaviour.

9. Theories of evolutionary processes include the idea that natural selection operates on the group as well as individuals, sociobiology, which emphasises the gene as the unit of natural selection, and approaches which emphasise the importance of genes, learning and environment in producing behavioural diversity.

LEARNING OBJECTIVES

1. **Courtship**
   The student shall be able to:
   - identify mechanisms involved in courtship rituals
   - describe theories of courtship
   - apply theories of courtship to specific examples

2. **Imprinting**
   The student shall be able to:
   - identify mechanisms involved in the process of imprinting
   - describe a study of imprinting
   - distinguish between critical and sensitive periods

3. **Attachment**
   The student shall be able to:
   - describe a study of attachment in monkeys
   - identify ethical considerations arising from investigations of attachment
   - evaluate the concept of imprinting as the model for all attachment

4. **Parental behaviour**
   The student shall be able to:
   - list stages of parental behaviour in monkeys
   - describe forms of parenting behaviour in animals
   - identify factors which can disturb or disrupt parental behaviour

5. **Social organisation**
   The student shall be able to:
   - describe a study of animal social organisation
   - outline factors which may influence dominance-based social organisation
   - identify sources of error in animal observation

6. **Territoriality**
   The student shall be able to:
   - identify different forms of territoriality
   - outline theories of territoriality
   - evaluate theories of territorial behaviour

7. **Aggression and reconciliation**
   The student shall be able to:
   - outline Lorenz's model of ritualised aggression
   - evaluate explanations of aggressive behaviour in animals
   - describe the concept of reconciliation

8. **Evolutionary theories**
   The student shall be able to:
   - describe different evolutionary theories
   - evaluate different theories of evolution
   - apply the concept of levels of explanation to animal behaviour

Courtship

1. Courtship rituals often involve a chain of _____ behaviour patterns

2. A courtship ritual which also protects the animal from danger is an example of:
(a) courtship ensuring pairing with the right species
(b) courtship as a fitness display
(c) courtship as strengthening pair-bonding
(d) courtship as permitting survival

3. The red deer's rut is an example of courtship as a _____

Imprinting

4. One of the first responses involved in imprinting is:
(a) following
(b) sexual attraction
(c) feeding
(d) attachment

5. Sluckin and Salzin showed that _____ young ducklings could extend the sensitive period

6. A critical period is:
(a) the usual time for something to happen
(b) the best possible time for something to happen
(c) the time something is most likely to happen
(d) the only time for something to happen

Attachment

7. Harlow used _____ mothers to investigate monkey attachments

8. Isolation experiments on infant monkeys are now considered unethical because they have lasting _____ and emotional effects

9. Studies of parent-infant _____ in humans show that not all attachments develop from imprinting

Parental behaviour

10. The second stage of parental behaviour in monkeys is the _____ stage

11. A rabbit's parental care lasts for approximately:
(a) 4 - 5 days
(b) 2 - 3 weeks
(c) 4 - 6 weeks
(d) 7 - 9 weeks

12. Maternal behaviour in monkeys has been shown to be affected by:
(a) lack of contact with other monkeys in adulthood
(b) lack of contact with other monkeys in infancy
(c) vegetarian diets
(d) lack of toys to play with

Social organisation

13. Rowell showed that baboons in a zoo
had hierarchical behaviour which was:
(a) flexible
(b) variable
(c) altruistic
(d) rigid

14. Remaining in one place to be fed may
have influenced _____ patterns
among the chimpanzees at the Gombe
Reserve

15. Projecting our own social assumptions
onto animal societies is an example of

_____

Territoriality

16. Defending a territory only during the
breeding period is _____
territoriality

17. Game theory approaches to
territoriality use:
(a) ethological observations
(b) experimental methods
(c) mathematical modelling
(d) projections from human society

18. The idea of territoriality as ensuring a
food reserve is uncertain because male
blackbirds:
(a) will allow another male to feed in
their territory
(b) will chase off all other blackbirds
(c) do not allow females to feed
(d) will allow another male to mate in
their territory

19. Lorenz's model of aggression was based on:
(a) the frustration-aggression model
(b) the social learning model
(c) the hydraulic model
(d) the humanistic model

20. Calhoun showed that _____ in rats increased aggression

21. Reconciliation is when two or more animals:
(a) restore the social balance after a fight
(b) fight to the death
(c) stop a fight when one is hurt
(d) involve others in a fight

22. The _____ approach suggests that the survival of an individual's genes is all that is important

23. Many popular versions of evolutionary theory have been criticised because:
(a) they only concern species development
(b) they do not consider females
(c) they are based on Lamarckian genetics
(d) they are derived from Darwin's ideas

24. Hinde argued that we must be cautious about extrapolating from animal to human behaviour because humans and animals have different _____ abilities

REVISION QUESTIONS

1. *Describe different types of dominance behaviour among primates*

2. *Outline the major forms of territoriality*

3. *What are the basic mechanisms of sociobiology?*

ESSAY QUESTIONS

1. *How far does imprinting provide an adequate explanation of the process of attachment?*

2. *Describe, giving specific examples, the major theories of courtship*

3. *How adequate are evolutionary concepts for explaining the behaviour of both animals and human beings?*

USEFUL FURTHER READING

Manning, A. & Dawkins, M. S. (1992) *An introduction to animal behaviour* (4th ed.) Cambridge: Cambridge University Press

Lea, S. E. G. (1984) *Instinct, environment and behaviour* London: Methuen

Archer, J. (1988) *The behavioural biology of aggression* Cambridge: Cambridge University Press

CHAPTER 23   ANIMAL COMMUNICATION

The key issues
This chapter is concerned with the question of animal communication. It begins by looking at the ways that animals receive and transmit information, including the dances used by honey bees, the voluntary and involuntary communications made by frogs, birdsong, and the songs of whales and dolphins.

The chapter then goes on to consider possible evolutionary precursors to human language, including the question of whether animals have "words" to stand for natural concepts, and whether they are able to communicate information about items not in the immediate environment. It concludes by evaluating some of the research which has specifically aimed to teach animals human-type languages.

Chapter summary

1. Animal communication can take place using a number of sensory modes, including the visual, olfactory, tactile, and auditory modes. Olfactory communication can include the use of pheromones. Bright argued that sound is the most flexible form of animal communication.

2. Honey bees communicate the location of food sources by dancing when they return to the hive. Features of the dance inform other bees about the direction and distance of the food source.

3. Male frog calls have to strike a balance between attracting females and not informing predators as to their location. Bats can use echolocation as a form of communication as well as a hunting tool.

4. Birdsong can serve both territorial and courtship functions. It is often partly learned and partly inherited. Marler identified a number of parallels between birdsong and speech, which may suggest an evolutionary link.

5. Humpback whales sing a distinctive and complicated song, which changes gradually during the course of the year and may be associated with courtship. Dolphins use a variety of sounds, which appear to aid social co-ordination as well as communicating specific messages.

6. Vervet monkeys and ground squirrels use different sounds to identify specific types of predator. Marler suggested that these reflected inbuilt natural categories, which might provide evolutionary links to human cognition and language use.

7. Chimpanzees use both sounds and visual signals to communicate in the wild, and may be able to communicate about distant objects such as food or snakes to one another.

8. There have been some attempts to teach chimpanzees, gorillas, and dolphins human languages. The methods used involve teaching sign language or special artificial languages. Some of the animals involved have invented new words and appear to see language as a communicative tool.

9. There is debate about how far attempts to teach animals human languages have been successful. The debate appears to be more about the special nature of the human being than about the capacity of the animals concerned.

LEARNING OBJECTIVES

1. **Forms of communication**
   The student shall be able to:
   - outline key features of communication
   - describe different forms of communication
   - compare different forms of communication

2. **Honey bee communication**
   The student shall be able to:
   - outline the process of bee communication
   - describe a study of bee communication
   - identify aspects of the bee's communication code

3. **Frogs and bats**
   The student shall be able to:
   - describe a study of communication in frogs or bats
   - identify processes of communication / prey location in frogs or bats
   - outline adaptive and maladaptive features of frogs and bat behaviour

4. **Birdsong**
   The student shall be able to:
   - outline the major functions of birdsong
   - describe features of birdsong and its development
   - identify parallels between birdsong and language

5. **Whales and dolphins**
   The student shall be able to:
   - describe whale and dolphin vocalisations
   - identify apparent functions of whale and dolphin sounds
   - describe a study of whale or dolphin communication

6. **Natural "words"**
   The student shall be able to:
   - describe a study of animal "words"
   - identify developmental processes in animal "words"
   - outline Marler's theory of natural categories

7. **Chimpanzee communication**
   The student shall be able to:
   - list different types of chimpanzee communication
   - identify functions of types of chimpanzee communication
   - describe a study of chimpanzee communication

8. **Teaching animals language**
   The student shall be able to:
   - outline different methods of teaching language to animals
   - describe a study involving teaching animals language
   - outline major arguments in the debate on animal language

OBJECTIVE QUESTIONS

Forms of communication

1. _____ is when both sender and receiver benefit from a communication

2. Olfactory communication involves:
(a) sight
(b) smell
(c) touch
(d) sound

3. Bright argued that _____ is better than visual signals because it can travel further

Bee communication

4. Honey bees communicate the location of nectar by:
(a) buzzing
(b) flying
(c) dancing
(d) humming

5. Von Frisch used _____ water to study how honey bees communicated the whereabouts of nectar

6. The "waggling" part of the bee's dance indicates that food is:
(a) 10m away
(b) 30m away
(c) 50m away
(d) 100m away or more

Frogs and bats

7. Barclay and Fenton studied little brown bats by:
(a) taking night-time photographs
(b) feeding them frogs
(c) observing them in cages
(d) recording the sounds they made

8. Pye showed that bats use more than one kind of _____

9. Tuttle and Ryan showed that frogs were more often caught by bats:
(a) if the weather was cloudy
(b) if the weather was windy
(c) if the weather was rainy
(d) if it was the early evening

Birdsong

10. The main function of the dawn chorus appears to be _____

11. Birds seem to develop regional song variations through _____

12. Both birdsong and language are centred on the _____ side of the brain

Cetaceans

13. Whistling was one of the first _____ sounds to be investigated

14. Humpback whales usually only sing during their _____

15. Norris and Dohl studied dolphins in:
(a) The North Atlantic
(b) the Bahamas
(c) the Barrier Reef
(d) Hawaii

Animal "words"

16. Cheyney and Seyfarth found that vervet monkeys have different alarm calls for leopards, eagles and _____

17. Young vervet monkeys differ from adults in that they:
(a) make louder sounds
(b) make more sounds
(c) over-generalise alarm calls
(d) under-generalise alarm calls

18. Marler argued that words for natural categories would be:
(a) species-specific
(b) over-generalised
(c) under-generalised
(d) common to all primates

Chimpanzee communication

19. The chimpanzee call which consists of "hoo" sounds and ends with a loud "waaa" is known as a _____

20. A soft bark may signal a mild _____ from one chimpanzee to another

21. Menzel showed that chimpanzees would ignore _____ chimpanzees who knew where food was hidden

Teaching animals

22. Washoe was taught American _____ language

23. Herman, Richards and Wolz taught _____ to respond to a special language

24. Terrace argued that animals who seemed to be using sign language were really only learning by _____ conditioning

REVISION QUESTIONS

1.   *Describe different types of animal sensory reception*

2.   *What do we know about honey bee communication?*

3.   *Outline the main features of cetacean communication*

ESSAY QUESTIONS

1.   *Discuss the nature and functions of birdsong. How similar is birdsong to human language?*

2.   *Do animals have "words"? Evaluate this question, drawing on forms of animal communication which have not been specifically taught by human beings*

3.   *Is it possible to teach non-human animals to use language?*

USEFUL FURTHER READING

Pearce, J. M. (1987) *An introduction to animal cognition* Hove: Lawrence Erlbaum Associates

Schusterman, R. J., Thomas, J. A. & Wood, F. G. (1986) *Dolphin cognition and behaviour: a comparative approach* Hillsdale, N.J.: Lawrence Erlbaum Associates

Hayes, N. (1994) *Principles of comparative psychology* Hove: Lawrence Erlbaum Associates

CHAPTER 24   METHODS AND ETHICS IN PSYCHOLOGY

The key issues

The aim of this chapter is to encourage students to reappraise and re-evaluate the psychological research which they have studied throughout the book. It begins by looking at the fundamental criteria used to evaluate psychological research, before going on to brief descriptions of research methods, with examples of each drawn from the main text.

The chapter then goes on to consider ethical issues in psychology, identifying major issues, and inviting the student to re-evaluate the research described in earlier chapters. It examines the questions raised by respecting research participants, avoiding personal distress, the use of animals in research, and the social responsibility of science.

Chapter summary

1. Psychologists use many different methods of studying people. There are three criteria which are important in collecting psychological evidence: validity, reliability, and generalisability.

2. Quantitative approaches to collecting psychological evidence have included the use of experiments, observations, questionnaires and surveys, and meta-analysis. Case studies and observations may also give qualitative data.

3. There are many different forms of qualitative analysis, which include looking at how people perform tasks or tell stories, and particularly the use of interviews and discourse analysis. Ethogenic research emphasises the understanding of social experience in the form of episodes and accounts.

4. Ethical issues in psychology have become very important in recent years. They are based around respect for the participant in the research programme. The use of deception or other forms of manipulation in psychological research is no longer considered acceptable unless there is very good reason for it.

5. Psychologists are required to avoid causing personal distress or discomfort to their research participants. This means that much research conducted in the past is no longer ethically acceptable.

6. Animal studies in psychology may be ranged along a continuum from strictly-confined laboratory investigations to free-ranging ethological studies. Studies involving vivisection are no longer considered to be acceptable except in very special cases.

7. Consideration of ethical issues also includes wider social questions, such as the social responsibility of science, and questions of multiculturalism and social respect for all human beings.

LEARNING OBJECTIVES

1. **Criteria for psychological evidence**
   The student shall be able to:
   - define terms relating to criteria for evidence
   - identify issues of validity, reliability and generalisability
   - apply the concept of levels of explanation to psychological research

2. **Research methods**
   The student shall be able to:
   - define terms relating to methods of research
   - describe the major research methods
   - identify examples of methods of study in psychological research

3. **Qualitative analysis**
   The student shall be able to:
   - list different types of interviews
   - describe different techniques of qualitative analysis
   - identify examples of qualitative methods in psychological research

4. **Ethics and deception**
   The student shall be able to:
   - identify factors leading to concern about ethical issues
   - list ethical guidelines for psychologists
   - apply criteria for ethical decisions to psychological research

5. **Avoiding personal distress**
   The student shall be able to:
   - outline relevant ethical criteria for psychological research
   - describe specific examples of ethically significant past research
   - evaluate psychological research in terms of ethical principles

6. **Animal studies**
   The student shall be able to:
   - identify different types of research into animal behaviour
   - list ethical guidelines for animal research
   - evaluate past research in terms of ethical issues

7. **Social responsibility**
   The student shall be able to:
   - describe the principles of social responsibility of science
   - outline applications of cultural awareness in psychological research
   - evaluate past psychological work in terms of social responsibility of science

OBJECTIVE QUESTIONS

Criteria

1. Measuring what you are intending to measure is known as _____

2. Validity and _____ need to be balanced in a psychological study

3. Looking into neurological mechanisms of imprinting is an example of research at the:
(a) cultural level of explanation
(b) social level of explanation
(c) physiological level of explanation
(d) behavioural level of explanation

Research methods

4. The _____ variable is the variable which is manipulated by the experimenter

5. Integrating the results of a large number of studies is known as a:
(a) survey
(b) case study
(c) experiment
(d) meta-analysis

6. Brown and Harris used _____ to study depression in housewives

Qualitative analysis

7. Interviews in which interviewer and interviewee have different goals are known as _____ interviews

8. Harré's ethogenic approach includes episode analysis and _____ analysis

9. Discourse analysis was used by:
(a) Milgram
(b) Lutz
(c) Bandura and Walters
(d) Schaffer and Emerson

Ethics and deception

10. Concern about ethical issues came partly from the way that research participants were being:
(a) manipulated
(b) selected
(c) refused payment
(d) ignored

11. The second BPS guideline for research is that participants should give their _____ consent

12. Hofling's study of obedience can be justified because:
(a) the information was important and could not be obtained any other way
(b) the information did not involve normal research participants
(c) the nurses in the study were all identified
(d) nurses expect to be ordered around by doctors

Avoiding distress

13. Ethical criteria for psychological research include not causing personal

_____

14. Watson and Raynor induced a _____ in little Albert

15. Which of these ethical concerns did
not apply to studies which manipulated
levels of self-esteem:
(a) they could cause undue distress
(b) they involved deception
(c) they did not involve informed consent
(d) they did not debrief participants

Animal studies

16. Studying animals in their natural
habitat is known as _____

17. The fourth BPS guideline for research
with animals is that:
(a) researchers must comply with UK law
(b) researchers must use the minimum
number of animals
(c) researchers must attend to species needs
(d) researchers should use field methods
where possible

18. Harlow's studies of attachment in
monkeys have been criticised because:
(a) they did not use enough monkeys
(b) the monkeys developed stomach ulcers
(c) they liked the towelling model better
(d) they caused lasting damage to the
animals

Social responsibility

19. Social responsibility of science
emphasises that scientists do not exist in a
_____ -free universe

20. Cultural awareness in psychological
research includes becoming more aware of
ethnocentric bias in _____ research
participants

21. Goddard's views on _____ led
directly to restrictive immigration laws in
America

REVISION QUESTIONS

1.   *Briefly describe, giving examples, the four main types of validity*

2.   *Describe three different ways of undertaking qualitative analysis*

3.   *What are the central concepts in ethical issues with regard to research with animals?*

ESSAY QUESTIONS

1.   *How far is the experimental method an appropriate technique for studying human behaviour?*

2.   *Are animal studies any use to psychologists?*

3.   *"Taking ethical issues seriously requires a complete re-think of psychological methodology". Discuss*

USEFUL FURTHER READING

Coolican, H. (1990) *Research methods and statistics in psychology*
London: Hodder & Stoughton

Robson, C. (1993) *Real world research* Oxford: Blackwell

Harré, R. (1993) *Social being* (2nd ed.) Oxford: Blackwell

ANSWERS TO OBJECTIVE QUESTIONS

Chapter 1
1. behaviourist	2. b	3. behaviourism
4. Wundt	5. c	6. introspectionism
7. operant	8. stimulus-response	9. a
10. Gestalt	11. species	12. d
13. truth	14. humanistic	15. b
16. d	17. b	18. cognition
19. a	20. non-experimental	21. ethological
22. d	23. lifespan	24. natural
25. a	26. c	27. reductionist

Chapter 2
1. similarity	2. d	3. constancy scaling
4. template	5. b	6. c
7. c	8. computational	9. d
10. d	11. social	12. a
13. a	14. perceptual defence	15. perceptual set
16. hypothesis	17. generalise	18. b
19. decrement	20. c	21. Yerkes-Dodson
22. dichotic	23. d	24. cocktail party
25. anticipatory	26. d	27. sampling

Chapter 3
1. nonsense	2. a	3. ecological
4. meaningful	5. d	6. rumours
7. anterograde	8. c	9. interference
10. 7+/-2	11. b	12. levels
13. a	14. processed	15. football
16. c	17. a	18. attention
19. flashbulb	20. a	21. b

Chapter 4
1. non-verbal	2. c	3. attributional
4. thought	5. strong	6. Japanese
7. particularistic	8. c	9. black
10. accent	11. b	12. d
13. stimulus	14. a	15. competence
16. d	17. speed	18. skilled
19. c	20. d	21. disembedded
22. acquired	23. verbal	24. a

Chapter 5

1. schemata	2. b	3. schema/ script
4. stimulus-response	5. d	6. c
7. b	8. social	9. b
10. Einstellung	11. a	12. brainstorming
13. entrapment	14. representativeness	15. illusory
16. c	17. protocols	18. a
19. interactive	20. c	21. c

Chapter 6

1. age	2. third	3. d
4. c	5. a	6. eugenics
7. c	8. specific	9. g factor
10. heritability	11. a	12. assistants
13. c	14. b	15. biological
16. reliable	17. d	18. environmental
19. 7	20. c	21. brain damage
22. automatisation	23. experiential	24. d

Chapter 7

1. phrenology	2. somatotypes	3. b
4. repression	5. refutability	6. b
7. c	8. psychometric	9. temperament
10. reductionist	11. b	12. imitation
13. play	14. b	15. self-efficacy
16. d	17. personal constructs	18. b
19. c	20. A	21. control
22. ipsative	23. individualism	24. c

Chapter 8

1. physical	2. d	3. unscientific
4. b	5. psychotic	6. a
7. attention	8. electrical	9. chemotherapy
10. responsible	11. problems in living	12. c
13. b	14. reliability	15. social
16. d	17. c	18. autonomy
19. c	20. b	21. family
22. manic / bipolar	23. learned helplessness	24. d
25. bulimia	26. a	27. psychoanalytic

Chapter 9

1. conflicts	2. a	3. d
4. a	5. habituation	6. b
7. self-actualisation	8. a	9. non-directive
10. insecure	11. b	12. choice
13. appraisal	14. situational/external	15. c
16. tight	17. d	18. restructuring
19. awareness	20. transaction	21. c
22. pseudomutuality	23. a	24. d

Chapter 10

1. b	2. brain	3. autonomic
4. b	5. phantom	6. thalamus
7. sensory	8. d c a b	9. b
10. a	11. c	12. anti-anxiety
13. d	14. proactive	15. follow-up
16. angular gyrus	17. c	18. b d a c
19. b	20. electrical	21. left
22. right	23. a	24. d

Chapter 11

1. zeitgebers	2. c	3. b
4. d	5. 4	6. before
7. melatonin	8. EEG	9. b
10. d	11. a	12. b
13. EEG	14. d	15. stimulation
16. synapse	17. stimulant	18. d
19. pain	20. hidden observer	21. c
22. auto-hypnosis	23. a	24. memory

Chapter 12

1. d	2. secondary	3. actualisation
4. hypothalamus	5. c	6. obese
7. exploration	8. extinguish	9. b
10. d	11. physiological	12. respect
13. d	14. c	15. a
16. resistance	17. monkeys	18. biofeedback
19. b	20. a	21. facial
22. c	23. limerence	24. d

Chapter 13
1. self-esteem
2. c
3. parental
4. representatives
5. d
6. b
7. Japanese
8. one
9. a
10. physical
11. c
12. rejection
13. social exchange
14. b
15. b
16. diversity
17. a
18. d
19. liking
20. stimulation
21. c
22. chronic
23. attention
24. c

Chapter 14
1. c
2. eyebrow flash
3. gestures
4. power
5. rituals
6. d
7. central
8. prophecy
9. c
10. person
11. d
12. scripts
13. a
14. situational/external
15. distinctiveness
16. a
17. relevance
18. validity
19. representations
20. figurative
21. individual

Chapter 15
1. increased
2. b
3. audience
4. sanction
5. riskier
6. b
7. d
8. b
9. c
10. a
11. consistency
12. compliance
13. nurses
14. c
15. a
16. altruistic
17. a
18. diffusion of responsibility
19. immediacy
20. reference
21. d
22. thanatos
23. football fans
24. c

Chapter 16
1. readiness
2. attitudes
3. d
4. affective
5. d
6. a
7. a
8. tension
9. b
10. assimilation
11. c
12. ratings/judgements
13. source
14. attitudes
15. b
16. psychoanalytic
17. Holland
18. c
19. accentuation
20. categorisation
21. d
22. a
23. summer camp
24. conflict

Chapter 17

1. Moro
2. leftovers
3. b
4. object
5. peek-a-boo
6. a
7. circular reaction
8. d
9. fine-tuning
10. a
11. decentre
12. assimilation
13. c
14. b
15. metacognition
16. c
17. hierarchical
18. d
19. focussing
20. automatisation
21. schema

Chapter 18

1. c
2. intelligent
3. stress
4. transactions
5. imitated
6. b
7. despair
8. low
9. b
10. neglect
11. a
12. continuity
13. b
14. Smarties box
15. c
16. c
17. emotional
18. autistic
19. c
20. autonomous
21. conventional

Chapter 19

1. vicarious
2. d
3. self-fulfilling prophecy
4. expectations
5. b
6. expectations
7. c
8. externally
9. families
10. d
11. metacommunication
12. surplus energy
13. a
14. a
15. c
16. d
17. learned
18. critical period
19. a
20. egocentricity
21. Bruner
22. cognitive
23. a
24. cognitive
25. b
26. verbal
27. d

Chapter 20

1. reciprocal
2. agents
3. social
4. regression
5. d
6. b
7. moratorium
8. initiative vs guilt
9. d
10. c
11. seasons
12. family
13. health / physical
14. a
15. b
16. denial
17. d
18. talk
19. intelligence / IQ
20. b
21. motivation
22. a
23. activity
24. a

Chapter 21
1. mechanisms
2. c
3. a
4. d
5. phylogeny
6. DNA
7. practised / learned
8. d
9. red
10. displacement
11. action-specific
12. consummatory stimulus
13. discrimination
14. c
15. predict
16. secondary
17. a
18. immediately
19. latent
20. gorillas/apes
21. d
22. critical
23. mobbing
24. b

Chapter 22
1. innate/inherited
2. d
3. fitness display
4. a
5. isolating
6. d
7. surrogate
8. social
9. interaction
10. ambivalent
11. b
12. b
13. d
14. dominance
15. anthropomorphism
16. seasonal
17. c
18. a
19. c
20. crowding
21. a
22. sociobiological
23. b
24. cognitive

Chapter 23
1. mutuality
2. b
3. sound
4. c
5. lavender
6. d
7. d
8. echolocation
9. a
10. territorial
11. learning
12. left
13. dolphin
14. mating season
15. d
16. snakes
17. c
18. a
19. pant-hoot
20. threat
21. stranger
22. sign / deaf & dumb
23. dolphins
24. operant

Chapter 24
1. validity
2. reliability
3. c
4. independent
5. d
6. interviews
7. hostile
8. account
9. b
10. a
11. informed
12. a
13. distress
14. phobia
15. d
16. ethology
17. b
18. d
19. value
20. selecting/sampling
21. intelligence/IQ

The following is an attempt to give you some idea of the kind of criteria which can be used when marking essays. Each essay, in this scheme, is marked out of 25, since this reflects common practice in many A level examination boards. University degree courses frequently have their own policies with regard to essay marking, but a glance at the criteria being applied here may nonetheless be helpful to a new lecturer.

Structure	Content	Theory/Evaluation
This sector of the marks is concerned with introducing and concluding essays appropriately; and with organising arguments and sequencing information sensibly, in a way which aids analysis or helps arguments to develop.	*This sector of the marks is given for knowing the actual information which has to be covered: psychological "facts", studies, theories, and so on.*	*This sector of the marks is given for producing appropriate criticisms of methods used or approaches adopted, for showing awareness of general perspectives and issues, and for applying theories appropriately to psychological evidence.*
Marks available	**Marks available**	**Marks available**
Up to **7** marks	Up to **10** marks	Up to **8** marks
This breaks down as:	**This can be banded as:**	**This can be banded as:**
Introduction up to **2** marks	*Full knowledge of material, describing relevant points clearly* up to **10** marks	*Competent evaluation of material, including general issues as well as relevant criticisms* up to **8** marks
Internal structure up to **3** marks	*Some knowledge of relevant material, but with gaps or errors* up to **7** marks	*Attempts at appropriate criticisms / perspectives / analysis but still leaving something to be desired* up to **5** marks
Conclusion up to **2** marks	*Very basic mention of the material* up to **3** marks	*Only very basic or simplistic criticisms* up to **2** marks